MW01049071

VIBRANT INDIA

VIBRANT INDIA

FRESH VEGETARIAN RECIPES
from Bangalore to Brooklyn

CHITRA AGRAWAL

photography by Erin Scott
illustrations by Karen Vasudev

TEN SPEED PRESS
California | New York

For my parents,
Prathima and Vishwani Agrawal,
and the city where they met,
Bangalore.

In loving memory of
Shantha Arakere Kumar.

INTRODUCTION

For as long as I can remember, my family has taken part in the "sport" of picking vegetables and fruits. I snapped the shot below of my grandmother, great aunt, mother, and father surrounding an unassuming guava vendor as they scrutinized his stock looking for the perfect fruit. This has been a familiar scene for me all my life, and one that has shaped the style of Indian home cooking I prepare—reliant on fresh produce and ingredients.

To many, the mention of Indian food elicits visions of heavy, all-you-can-eat lunch buffet specials, cream-laden curries, naan, and, of course, chicken tikka masala, which ironically was invented in the United Kingdom. These dishes form a myopic view of India's cuisine, however. What's missing is a vast range of cooking tradtitions that have existed in Indian homes for hundreds of years. All are distinctly flavorful in their own right, but South Indian food, and in particular the Brahmin vegetarian diet followed by my ancestors on my mother's side, is also known for its emphasis on health. I share these favorite, time-tested family recipes here with you.

As a lifelong vegetarian, I have answered many questions from people about where I get my protein and whether I get enough of it in my diet. Though it may not fit into the traditional meat-and-potato model of Western cooking, the combination of rice, legumes, vegetables, and yogurt that I grew up eating on a daily basis forms a complete and satisfying meal and is just as packed with protein. One could argue that it's also more healthful and flavorful thanks to the array of spices employed in its preparation. There's a reason why Chef Anthony Bourdain, a notorious carnivore, embraces a vegetarian diet while traveling in India: "This is one of the few places in the world where I could eat vegetarian every day and still be happy," he has said.

Until recently, restaurants and cookbooks focusing on North Indian cooking have been most prevalent in the U.S. market,

My paternal great aunt, grandmother, mom, and dad shopping for guava in Delhi.

which makes sense, as the first Indian immigrants to settle in America in the early 1900s were from North India. I am often asked to clarify the difference between North and South Indian cooking because my mother is from Bangalore, a city in the southern state of Karnataka, and my father grew up in Allahabad and Delhi, cities in the northern state of Uttar Pradesh. As a result, my parents ate quite distinct cuisines, despite the fact that they were both vegetarian and Hindu.

Generally speaking, the foundation of South Indian cooking relies heavily on rice and lentils, as opposed to the breads and curry preparations of the North. Fresh coconut and curry leaves are generously used by South Indian home cooks but are relatively absent from North Indian fare. Dishes such as *dosas* (rice and lentil crepes, page 38), *idlis* (steamed rice and lentil cakes, page 48), and *huli* or *sambar* (vegetable and lentil stew, page 131) are all South Indian. Much of what you eat in U.S. restaurants, like naan, samosas, and curries such as *palak paneer* (spinach and cheese) are North Indian. Both cuisines also have their own spice mixtures and powders. Garam masala is commonly used in the North, and *saarina pudi* or *rasam* powder is found in the South. Amchur, a dried green mango powder, is used as a souring agent in North Indian curries, while tamarind flavors many South Indian stews. The hot drink of choice is even different. In the North, a meal is followed by tea or chai, while in the South, one drinks coffee made with chicory. Of course, this comparison of North and South Indian cooking does not even begin to scratch the surface of the diversity of India's cuisine. This is why studying the foods of India is so fascinating: There is always something new to learn.

Getting to know these foods also has a practical purpose. It's no secret that Americans today are drawn toward a more vegetable-centric way of eating for matters of health and sustainability, not to mention wishing to incorporate more spices like turmeric, a natural antiseptic, into their diets to promote wellness. Twenty-six percent of Americans consciously chose to eat less meat in 2015. The value of drawing on plant-based food traditions from around the world has become more relevant today than ever.

The South Indian home cooking of my mother's family is deeply rooted in the strict vegetarian customs of Hindu Brahmins and healthful practices of ayurveda, an ancient Hindu medicinal approach encompassing diet, yoga, and meditation that originated in India. For centuries, the region has honed its cuisine for optimum flavor, nutrition, and sensory appeal. It is both light and fresh while possessing the ability to carry some serious heat, thus creating a cuisine rich in unique and complex flavors. Grains, legumes, vegetables, fruits, and spices form the cornerstone of this cuisine, known for its inventiveness and diversity. The dishes naturally lend themselves to vegetarian, vegan, and gluten-free diets—from *uttapam* (page 42), a savory lentil and rice pancake served up at the always-packed Saravana Bhavan restaurant in Manhattan, to the refreshing *kosambri* salad (page 61) made with shredded carrots, soaked lentils, coconut, lemon, and fried spices in Bangalorean homes.

A defining trademark of Karnataka cuisine, similar to other ancient cuisines from around the world, is to make the best use of what the season has to offer, which is what is usually most plentiful in the markets at any given time. Using local ingredients is how my family has been cooking Indian food for generations, dating back to the farmland in our ancestral village of Arakere. This practice has been ingrained in my lifestyle from an early age, and it's one I carry out today at the Greenmarket and as a farm share member.

Family Ties

This book is an ode to my mother and her city. Founded in 1537 by Kempe Gowda, Bangalore, or Bengaluru as it is referred to in the local language of Kannada, is the fourth most populous city in India. Home to a predominantly Hindu population in addition to Christian, Muslim, and Jain minorities, the city is the capital of Karnataka state. Located on the Deccan Plateau in South India, three thousand feet above sea level, Bangalore boasts one of the most temperate climates in the country and is dotted with a number of freshwater lakes and green vegetation.

Bangalore was historically referred to as the Garden City of India because of its abundant public gardens and large bungalows surrounded by lush greenery. Fruits and vegetables grew easily thanks to the favorable climate, and the area abounded with orchards. In the 1940s, my grandfather purchased a Bangalore property dotted with apple trees growing the Rome Beauty variety. In the 1980s, the city experienced a population boom, and in recent years it has transitioned into a rapidly growing tech capital, housing IT professionals from all over India and outposts for major international technology companies. Because of this influx, Bangalore has become more urban and cosmopolitan, but there are still pockets that harken back to its greener days.

My maternal grandparents originally hailed from southern Karnataka—my grandmother from an affluent family in the city of Mysore and my grandfather from roots in the farming village of Arakere. My mother's great-grandfather, Vasudevaiah, started out poor but eventually became a prosperous farmer who grew coconuts, mangoes, jackfruit, sorghum, tamarind, red chiles, and rice on more than 150 acres of land, which to this day produces those same crops. Much of the food consumed was hearty, including grains such as *ragi* or finger millet and coarse,

unpolished rice with its inner husk intact that stuck with you while working long hours in the fields. In those days, staying healthy through food and good hygiene was of utmost importance, and the merits of homeopathy and naturopathy were tested each day. My mother's grandmother, Kalakka, was an apothecary of sorts, concocting herbal medicines, root elixirs, and medicinal drinks like *shunti* (ginger) coffee, which would be dispensed to family members to treat different ailments, such as indigestion and throat infections, and to help in recovery after childbirth.

In 1963, my mother and father met in Bangalore while studying electrical engineering at the Indian Institute of Science. My parents have what is referred to as a "love marriage" in India, one that was not arranged by their family and parents. Although they came from different parts of the country, did not share the same mother tongue (my father's is Hindi, while my mother's is Kannada), and were of different Hindu castes (my mother is Brahmin and my father is Vaishya), they agreed on one thing—well, two things—the importance of being vegetarian and their love for each other. They left Bangalore in 1968 to pursue higher education in the United States, where they eventually married and started a family, settling in New Jersey. On our annual trips back to Bangalore, we stayed in the Kumara Park house where my mother grew up. In 1990, they built their own house in Bangalore, not far from my grandparents' home.

My ties to India go back generations. My parents left India in 1968, eventually marrying in Illinois (left) and settling in New Jersey (right).

South Indian Food Traditions

The community that my mother's family belongs to in South India is referred to as Hoysala Karnataka Brahmins, a group of Hindu Brahmins dating back to the time of the Hoysala Empire, which ruled Karnataka from the tenth to fourteenth centuries. By tradition, Brahmins adhere to practices of the Hindu priest class, which include rituals that promote healthful balance in the body and cleanliness in the household. For instance, my great-grandmother Kalakka would not enter the kitchen to prepare food under any circumstances until she had taken a bath. I come from a long line of strict vegetarians who followed a sattvic or yogic diet that is referred to in the ancient Hindu text Bhagavad Gita as a way to purify one's existence, gain strength and harmony in the body, and lead a peaceful and satisfying life without inflicting harm on others.

This particular South Indian diet comprises seasonal vegetables and fruits and unprocessed whole grains, nuts, seeds, oils, and dairy, all said to be foods acceptable for offering to Hindu gods. According to the ancient Hindu medical system of ayurveda, sattvic is just one of three *gunas* or categories of food and being. The other two are tamasic, which is considered to be destructive and includes foods that are supposed to sedate the body, such as meat, fish, eggs,

My mother's family; she is second from the left.

onion, garlic, and alcohol; and rajasic, which is associated with passion and includes stimulants such as caffeine, overly spicy or salty food, and chocolate.

Until about the 1930s, orthodox Brahmins, including my great-grandfathers, did not eat rajasic foods such as tomatoes, carrots, or radishes, on account of their bright color. Of course, as culinary traditions from different parts of the world and country found their way to South India, these strict dietary rules and categories started to loosen somewhat, but to this day my mother never handles garlic in her kitchen. The traditional recipes I modeled the ones in this book after used no onion or garlic, and instead relied more on the spice asafetida, or *hing*, which, when fried in oil or ghee, imparts a similar pungent aroma and flavor.

For many years, my grandparents' household was filled to the brim with their own children (seven) and extended family. As a result, my grandmother was in charge of cooking three meals a day for up to twenty people at times. From accounts of family members, she was an amazing force to be reckoned with in the kitchen. Her cooking was streamlined to produce large quantities of quickly prepared, delicious food that fit into a tight budget.

My mother grew up eating the quintessential South Indian food of Karnataka, a true celebration of vegetarian ingredients resulting in a perfect melding of sour, sweet, bitter, spicy, and savory flavors all on one plate. Often she would

A meal served on banana leaves at my parents' housewarming in Bangalore.

have a breakfast of *uppittu* (page 55), fluffy semolina porridge flavored with black mustard seeds, curry leaf, turmeric, dried red chiles, and coconut and cooked with a seasonal vegetable like *avarekai*, a bright green-and-yellow bean similar to edamame. A typical dinner for the family would consist of *sanna akki* (a short-grained rice) with *saaru* (a thin soup made with tomatoes, lentils, tamarind, and an intoxicating homemade powdered spice mixture, page 125) and *palya* (pages 80 to 82), a vegetable stir-fry made from produce bought that day from the market. Each meal ended with plain rice and yogurt or buttermilk to settle the stomach from the heat of the spices.

Even today, many of the food traditions my mother grew up with prevail. Hindu festivals play a large part in these traditions. Upon leaving a temple, you will be given *prasadam*—an offering of a bowl of buttery and sour tamarind, green mango, or lemon rice. Certain desserts are made for different holidays. For Ganesha Chaturthi, a Hindu festival honoring the elephant god Ganesh, *kadabu* (page 163), a sweet dumpling filled with coconut and jaggery, is prepared. On special occasions such as weddings in Karnataka, food is served and consumed in a particular order on a banana leaf. Sweets, sides, and condiments are served on top of the leaf, while main course items are served on the bottom portion. Usually, the meal begins with a sweet and ends with curd rice (page 110) or buttermilk (page 171). When this order is not followed, elders have been known to cause a ruckus!

On visits to Bangalore, I shop with my family for vegetables and fruits in Gandhi Bazaar or Malleshwaram market, or sometimes buy straight from the vegetable wallah, who shouts outside our house to signal her arrival. I stock up on readymade snacks like masala "Congress" peanuts (page 151) from Subbamma Stores, a hole-in-the-wall family-run shop in Gandhi Bazaar. I munch on spicy bitter gourd chips (page 152) fried fresh in front of me at one of the hot chip shops near our house or have a sweet cardamom biscuit from an Iyengar bakery in town. I can't leave without making a pit stop at some of the landmark Bangalorean restaurants I've been visiting since I was a kid, like Mahvelli Tiffin Rooms (MTR) or Vidyarthi Bhavan, which serve up Karnataka classics like masala dosa (page 42), idli (pages 45 and 48), and filter coffee (page 175). I love Veena's Stores, an old-school neighborhood stall that specializes in dishes like *shavige baath* (page 52), a bright turmeric-colored rice noodle dish. I soak up all of these Old World traditions while discovering new foods and ingredients that spark ideas in my kitchen back at home in Brooklyn.

My mother helping me drink fresh coconut water in her aunt's coconut grove in South India.

From Bangalore to Brooklyn

I was born and raised in the suburbs of New Jersey. Growing up, many things came full circle during our family vacations to Bangalore. At home, I'd watch my mother cook recipes sent by her mother and aunts back in India, and when we'd visit Bangalore, I'd get to eat those same recipes cooked by my grandmother, who would lovingly mix my food with her own hands. Trips always felt too short, but the experiences stayed with me: sampling local specialties served from stainless steel pails by waiters wearing traditional *dhotis*; visiting the site of my grandfather's old textile factory, where the foreman cut the top off a fresh coconut with a machete for me; and, of course, going to see different family members, who would stuff me silly with home cooking like *huggi* (page 112), a buttery rice and lentil dish similar to risotto. Many times, these meetings ended with a souvenir of a jar of homemade hot pickle or *uppinakayi*, a condiment of cut mango, lemon (page 185), or gooseberries preserved in a hot chile brine, pushed into my hands to smuggle back to the States.

In Jersey, mine was one of a few Indian families in a predominantly Catholic town of Italian- and Irish-Americans. Like many first-generation Indian-American kids, I straddled two worlds, one with my classmates from school and the other deeply entrenched in the culture of my parents' native India, with food as its most prominent aspect in our household. Compared to most homes in town, our kitchen

My preschool class; guess which one is me?

was filled with the aroma of fried spices, the distinct sound of a pressure cooker chugging away, and the warm glow of the oven light at night setting homemade yogurt. And just steps away was my room, resembling that of any American teen. I definitely went through awkward and self-conscious stages of feeling that I didn't fit in anywhere (lots of punk rock in those days!).

Over the years, I moved from wanting to fit in to feeling alright that I stood apart. A major shift occurred during my high school years in the 1990s, when I met and made some lifelong friends. Enticed by the aromas emanating from our kitchen, they would linger just long enough to get invited to dinner by my parents. As I watched them appreciate and enjoy our family meals (and later even prepare some of the dishes in their own kitchens), I saw that what we cooked at home was something special. Food was probably the first facet of my heritage that gave me great pride and even confidence in my identity, and that stayed with me. When I moved across the country to California for college, I longed for my family's home cooking. Each semester, my parents would fill my suitcase with frozen packets of homemade dishes, which I would carefully ration once back at my undergraduate apartment and share with my new friends at school.

Although food was always a central part of my life, I did not set out to make it my profession. In fact, after college I ended up in advertising, and a few years later, after getting an MBA, I was working in marketing at American Express. I was climbing the corporate ladder and was on a trajectory that was as far from food as you could get. Throughout those years, cooking gave me great comfort and a way to bond with family, but it never dawned on me that I could actually pursue it as a career.

My parents and their generation worked very hard to get the opportunity to study and gain employment in the sciences abroad, and it was incumbent on their children to make the most of those opportunities—to become doctors, lawyers, scientists, and businesspeople. In India, the chore of cooking was relegated to housewives or to hired cooks making a menial wage. It was not a way to make a living, especially for someone with my educational background.

Moreover, most culinary schools in the United States are geared toward European cuisines with none offering an education in vegetarian Indian home cooking, the food that captivated me most. Although I had grown up watching and helping my parents in the kitchen, I had never formally learned any of the recipes, and it was highly unlikely that previous generations in my family had either.

My mother had a little drawer in our kitchen where she kept a worn notebook and Aerogram letters containing recipes from her mother, which helped guide her cooking over the years. My father once told me that traditions are not merely passed down—it takes two. He could teach me procedures, but the techniques were up to me and could be learned only by doing. With that in mind, I set out to teach myself.

I started spending vacations at home following my mother and father around in the kitchen, observing, trying my hand at preparations, and taking copious notes. Trips to India became field studies, a way for me to gather as much knowledge as I could from elder family members. I spent nights at home poring over esoteric cookbooks I had brought back from India, cross-referencing recipes in old emails my mother had sent me when I was at college, and logging hours on the phone with my parents as I tried to figure out the precise texture for a soup I was re-creating from an old family recipe.

I began to codify ingredients: the sweetness of grated coconut and jaggery; the sourness of lemon juice, tamarind, and cooling yogurt; the bitterness of ginger, curry leaves, and black mustard seeds; the heat of black pepper and chile peppers; and just enough salt to hit the savory note. Over time, combinations came naturally, leading me back to that fine balance of sweet, sour, bitter, spicy, and savory flavors I grew up eating. In the process of learning these recipes, I was also learning more about my family's history, something I always felt distant from growing up in America.

In 2009 while living in Brooklyn, I began writing my food blog, *The ABCDs of Cooking*, as a way to document my family's recipes and stories. (ABCD is an acronym for American-Born Confused Desi, a term that refers to second-generation South Asians.) I worked hard to convert my mother's and aunts' recipes, which were often passed to me in the language of handfuls, pinches, or even just feel. I cooked and cooked and cooked until I got it right, relying on my taste memories for some dishes. I had purpose as I cooked because I realized I might be the last link to some of these family recipes, and I felt it was important to have a tangible record of them. Not surprisingly, many family members of my generation in the United States were not actively continuing these traditions in their own kitchens. I thought that if someone got curious somewhere down the line, this compilation would be a resource for them.

As I became more comfortable and even confident in my abilities, I began to experiment with my own versions of the dishes, using seasonal produce from local farms and different culinary influences. I was drawing from Italian flavors and even the greasy-spoon diners of my youth in New Jersey, Asian and Mexican flavors from my time in California, and my discoveries in my new home of New York City. I was blogging on a regular basis by then and realized that my readership had grown by leaps and bounds beyond my initial audience made up of my mom and a handful of friends. One thing led to another, and I was hired to teach my first private cooking class. Next, a chef friend of mine asked if I'd collaborate with her on a menu for an Indian-and-Mexican-themed supper club. And from that point on, I was hooked!

I started selling some of my prepared food at local markets in Brooklyn and teaching cooking classes around the city. I made it a point to focus on healthy, approachable recipes from my mother's side, dishes not usually found in Indian restaurants but that are staples in South Indian homes—*chitranna* (page 103), for example, a cheerfully bright yellow turmeric rice flavored with fried spices, peanuts, coconut, lemon, and cilantro. I was pleasantly surprised to see that the food I had grown up eating was resonating with a whole new group of people eager for nutritious vegetarian recipes with bold flavors. A project that began with a goal to preserve my family's culinary traditions had become a way for me to connect and engage with communities around me.

All the while, I still had my day job, now at a tech start-up. Momentum was building, and sleep was a luxury. Every free hour I devoted to developing a recipe for my blog, teaching a class, or selling at a market. My cooking had started to gain a following, and food writers were interested in my work too. I remember the first time my inbox filled up with email from friends and family all over the country

My dive into the food world, from the launch of Brooklyn Delhi to hosting pop-up dinners and teaching cooking classes.

after a story in the *New York Times* had my photo front and center serving my signature Indian tacos at an underground market held in a church basement in Brooklyn. I was on to something people liked, and most important, I was doing something I loved.

At that time, Brooklyn was in the midst of a food renaissance of sorts, and a subculture was forming apart from what was happening in the restaurant scene. It was a free-for-all of passionate and talented home cooks sharing their family recipes or just their innovative creations at markets, supper clubs, cook-offs, and just about anywhere people could eat. I felt I had found a community of like-minded individuals whom I could collaborate with and learn from.

I now partner with local farmers and food artisans to source and even grow special ingredients for my events and classes. At Tangra, a roving Indian-Chinese dinner series that I host with friend and cookbook author Diana Kuan, we serve vegetarian feasts featuring locally grown produce and brewed beer. Our first event was held at the Wyckoff Farmhouse Museum, where my friend and head farmer Jason Gaspar grew Indian vegetables from seeds I had brought back from Bangalore, and a small brewery in Long Island City, Queens, crafted a beer for us infused with curry leaves. I also work with New York farmers to source thousands of pounds of produce to make *achaars* at Brooklyn Delhi, the Indian condiments company that I co-own with my husband, Ben, a food packaging designer and artist.

At the same time we decided to launch Brooklyn Delhi, I also got a new job offer and landed the deal to write this cookbook. That was in 2013, and I was at a crossroads. There was no way I was going to be able to work at my day job, run a condiments business, and write a book. I couldn't ignore the fact that my interest in food had grown past a hobby. After much agonizing and scribbling of countless lists of pros and cons, I decided to leave my decade-long career in marketing to pursue food full-time. My parents and family were concerned, but I believed this was my chance. It was terrifying to give up my professional identity and the promise of a substantial weekly paycheck and benefits. To top it off, I was planning my wedding, in a town hundreds of miles from where I lived.

Looking back on the last few years, I can say that I've experienced some of my toughest days and have never worked harder, but I've also never enjoyed my work this much nor felt as fulfilled as I do now. Within a year of its launch, Brooklyn Delhi received critical acclaim from food editors at more than fifteen national publications, including *Saveur, The New York Times Magazine,* and Zagat, and our products were carried in over sixty stores nationwide, which further validated my decision to take the leap. I'm hopeful for the future and am beyond thrilled that you are now reading this book.

HOW TO USE THIS BOOK

Before you hit the kitchen, I highly recommend reviewing Indian Cooking Techniques and Tips on page 17. This section includes how to temper spices in oil, possibly the most important lesson I can teach you, in addition to tips on prepping ingredients and seasoning your dishes. To help you get started, I also introduce you to the South Indian pantry of ingredients (page 21) and useful kitchen tools for making Indian recipes (page 34). Last, I've included a starter grocery list of ingredients used most often in the book on page 207, plus where to buy them on page 206 and a resource on meal planning and sample menus on page 205.

Every recipe in the book is vegetarian, and each is labeled for the seasons and by dietary restrictions (V for vegan, G for gluten-free). Most of the recipes in the book are vegan and gluten-free and if not labeled as such can be easily modified. For example, where ghee is the only non-vegan ingredient used, you can substitute oil to make the dish vegan.

Recipes are titled in English with translations in Kannada, sometimes also in Tamil, another South Indian language, and on occasion in Hindi. Within recipes, I list Indian ingredients by how they are labeled at the Indian shop or online, which is usually in Hindi.

My approach to teaching cooking is focused on a flexibility of ingredients. I provide lots of substitutions in my notes, so if you don't have a particular vegetable, I have you covered with another one. Note that flavor and intensity of certain ingredients varies from brand to brand. For instance, if you are using a less-potent tamarind paste than mine, by all means add more than what I have specified to hit that sour note. Cooking temperatures and times may also vary, depending on your equipment, so just keep that in mind.

Last but not least, in no way do I want to imply that this book is a complete canon of South Indian cooking. The recipes are derived from age-old vegetarian culinary traditions from South India, but grounded in my reality as a busy city dweller. I stay true to traditional flavors but readily adapt recipes to my experience and to the ingredients and time I have on hand. The beauty of Indian home cooking is that it lends itself to creativity but has a distinct essence that permeates each iteration of a recipe. Learn from my interpretations and build on them further to make the recipes your own.

Indian Cooking Techniques and Tips

The Indian staples I cook in my home are quick and easy to prepare if you know a few basics, which I'll share with you here.

TEMPERING SPICES

The technique of tempering or frying spices in hot oil and adding them to a dish is at the heart of Indian cooking. Depending on the region, this technique may be referred to by different names such as *vagarne*, *oggarane*, *chaunk*, *tadka*, or *baghaar*, but the procedure is pretty much the same throughout India; only the types of oil and spices used will vary.

First, oil or butter is heated and when hot, spices are added one or two at a time in quick succession. This is when the functionality of the Indian spice box is most apparent. Since you are rapidly adding spices within seconds of each other, it is handy to have all of your spices in one place. Once in the hot oil, the spices may pop or sizzle, and their flavors will bloom and intensify. As many as five spices can be added to the oil, and then the hot oil is poured onto the yogurt, salad, or lentil dishes; other times vegetables or cooked rice are added to this oil to begin a recipe. When the seasoned oil is meant to finish a dish, the spices are usually fried in a tiny pot or small skillet.

Tempering is the single most important technique to learn, as it is used in almost every savory recipe in the book. I always tell my students not to worry if they burn the spices the first time; you can always discard those small amounts of spices and try again until you get it right. And when you get comfortable with the technique, you can apply it to more than just the recipes in this book. When I first taught my husband, Ben, how to temper spices, he applied the process to flavoring butter for his popcorn. His recipe was too good not to include here (page 147).

ROASTING SPICES

Many Indian homes do not have ovens, so roasting occurs predominantly on the stove. I prefer this method because I have more control over the roasting process, plus it is more energy efficient. I roast spices in a medium cast-iron skillet when I am making spice blends in bulk. Roasting releases the oils in the spices and brings out their full flavor and aroma. It can also completely change the flavor of a spice, as it does with coriander seeds, which go from grassy to citrusy. Many of the spice blends (pages 194 to 199) used in South Indian cooking are made by roasting whole spices, chiles, lentils, and curry leaves individually and then grinding them together. The process of roasting takes just minutes and will transform the flavor of your food.

To roast spices, I first heat my pan over low or medium-low heat. I add my spices and continuously move them around the pan with a wooden spatula, sometimes for less than a minute or up to five minutes, depending on the spice. The goal is to roast the spices evenly over a slow and consistent flame, which is why a heavy pan is preferred for the job. The slow heat coaxes out the spices' flavor and toasts them inside and out. As the spices are roasting, their aroma fills the air, becoming more fragrant until you can almost taste them. At this point, the spices are fully roasted and may have turned a shade darker. Once they are roasted, I place them on a plate to cool before grinding or storing them.

PREP

As mentioned previously, many Indian recipes call for a group of spices and fresh ingredients to be tempered in oil in quick succession. In order for this to go off without a hitch, you need to measure and gather them together by the stove before you begin the process. The combination most used in this book is black mustard seeds, asafetida, dried red chile peppers, and curry leaves. If you have those four items ready to go, you're all set to make the majority of the recipes in this book.

Besides the chopping of vegetables, the main ingredient that needs prepping in most of my recipes is grated coconut, which needs to be soaked in warm water for a few minutes if dried, or thawed if frozen. In a pinch you can zap frozen coconut in the microwave for fifteen seconds.

SALT, SEASON, AND TASTE—THEN TASTE SOME MORE

Spices in Indian cooking need a good amount of salt to bring them alive. Salt is the gateway to flavor. However, salt intensities, personal tastes, and dietary restrictions vary. I generally tend to taste and season dishes as I cook, sprinkling a little salt each time I add a vegetable to the pot, for instance. Taste your dish along the way and a final time before serving to decide whether you need one last bit of salt or a spritz of lemon juice to bring the dish to fruition. This is the best way to get to know your ingredients, understand how they behave, and, most important, figure out what you like best.

The South Indian Pantry

In this section I give detailed notes on the full range of ingredients for your South Indian pantry. These can be found at Indian shops and online (see the resources on page 206). A number of the ingredients listed here can also be found at grocery stores and specialty shops.

Spices

Spices are best preserved when stored in containers kept away from sunlight and heat.

Asafetida (hing): An extremely pungent resin derived from the sap of a plant similar to fennel. You can purchase it in chunks or as a powder. I usually purchase mine in chunks and grind them into a powder in my spice grinder. I buy the SSP brand, which is produced in Bangalore and sold in its pure form. The chunk form is hard to find, but powdered forms are abundant. Some of the powdered varieties may include trace amounts of wheat flour, but there are also gluten-free versions that contain rice flour, so check the labels closely. A little asafetida goes a long way, and most recipes call for just a pinch. I love passing an open container around my cooking classes and watching my students grimace. It's that intense! The beauty of asafetida is unlocked when it is fried in oil; it exudes an aroma and flavor similar to onion and garlic. Historically, it has been used in Brahmin and Jain kitchens, because these groups are prohibited from consuming onion and garlic for religious reasons. Asafetida is known to aid in digestion and is an ingredient in several ayurvedic medicines for this purpose. Although you could substitute onion and garlic, I highly recommend seeking this spice out. It's a game changer in the kitchen.

Black mustard seeds: Related to the yellow and brown mustard seeds used to make mustard, but more pungent. These seeds are a staple ingredient of South Indian cooking. They flavor most of the dishes in this book and are either fried in oil or ground raw and added to pastes. When added to hot oil, they pop as they release their moisture.

Black pepper: Native to South India and the original source of heat in dishes before the arrival of chiles to the region. Crushed black pepper is derived from pepper berries that have been dried. In South Indian dishes, black pepper is usually fried in ghee or butter to release its flavors and then ground or sometimes left whole and added to a variety of recipes or spice blends. Cumin seeds and black pepper are often paired together in dishes. This spice is best when freshly ground.

Cardamom: Native to India, green pods that grow on a plant related to ginger. Inside the pods are small, aromatic black seeds. Cardamom is used throughout India, but in South India it is primarily used in its ground form in desserts. The spice has a warm and subtly sweet and minty flavor. At Indian shops, you can purchase the whole pods, the seeds, or ground cardamom powder. I have not found much difference between the forms, but I prefer a finer ground in baked goods. If using the pods, break them open and grind the seeds in a mortar and pestle. The seeds can also be chewed raw as a breath freshener. Another variety of cardamom is black or brown and larger in size, but the recipes in this book use only the green variety.

Cinnamon: The dried inner bark of the upper branches of a tree native to South India and Sri Lanka. In South Indian cooking, the fragrant spice is fried in ghee and ground to make spice blends for different vegetable, lentil, and rice dishes. In spice blends I prefer to use the whole cinnamon stick versus the powder for a fresher flavor, but a 2-inch cinnamon stick is roughly equal to 1 teaspoon of powder.

Cloves: The dried, unopened flowers of a tropical evergreen tree from Indonesia with a sweet and spicy flavor. In South Indian cooking, cloves are usually fried in ghee and ground for use in spice blends to flavor lentil or rice dishes. Whole cloves can also be chewed raw as a breath freshener.

Coriander seeds: Round seeds from the cilantro plant that are roasted, ground, and used in spice blends in South Indian cooking. The spice has a grassy and citrusy flavor and is rich in antioxidants.

Cumin seeds: Small, light brown seeds of a member of the parsley family. The spice is used more in North Indian recipes but is found in South Indian recipes from time to time. When fried in oil, they provide a slightly nutty and smoky flavor to dishes.

Fenugreek seeds: Light brown, wrinkly seeds derived from the leafy fenugreek plant. When roasted and ground, the seeds take on a nutty and almost maplelike flavor (page 199). They are finicky, though, and will become bitter if fried in oil or roasted for a tad too long. I usually roast them until I can smell their nutty aroma yet they are still golden brown, but some prefer to roast them until they are a little reddish to get a tinge of bitterness. The spice is primarily used to flavor pickles and spice blends in South India. Fenugreek is known for increasing milk production for new mothers.

Saffron: Dried red stamens of crocus flowers with an intoxicating fragrance. Although saffron is grown in northern India, the saffron found in the United States is largely from Spain and Iran. It is laborious work to extract the threads from the flower, which accounts for saffron's expensive price tag. Like cardamom, saffron is used primarily in desserts in South India. It is quite potent—only a few strands are needed to flavor a whole dish. To release saffron's flavor, the threads are soaked in warm milk before being added to some recipes. It's important to purchase good-quality saffron in its thread form and not in a powdered state, as the spice is quite expensive and prone to adulteration. A good way to test whether your saffron is legitimate is to soak it in warm milk. If the milk turns a nice yellow color, and the threads retain their bright hue, the saffron is of good quality; if it turns reddish, you have been sold dyed threads.

Turmeric: A rhizome similar to ginger with a tough brown skin and bright orange-yellow flesh. It can be found in whole or powdered form and has an earthy, bitter taste and a slightly mustardlike smell. Its coloring is so potent that less than a spoonful will turn a whole pot of rice yellow. Curcumin, an antioxidant and the active component in turmeric, is thought to have healing properties with regard to cancer, Alzheimer's, and arthritis. Turmeric has long been used as an antiseptic in India and is used in pickling to prevent bacterial growth. It is also a digestive aid and is often added to lentils while they are cooking.

Chiles

Native to South America, chiles came to India by way of trade with the New World in the fifteenth century.

Dried whole red chiles: Slender, dark red, and usually broken in half and fried in oil or roasted and ground into spice blends. Chiles are the fruit of the capsicum plant and provide the heat for the majority of South Indian dishes. Numerous varieties of chiles are grown in India, and the state of Andra Pradesh in South India is the largest exporter of them. The most well-known chile from this region is referred to as the Guntur Sannam. I usually buy this variety or the bag labeled generically as "whole chillies" at an Indian shop. Dried cayenne or arbol chiles have a similar taste and heat and can be used in place of dried Indian red chiles.

Karnataka's contribution to chile production comes in the form of the Byadgi chile (photo on page 197), which is wrinkly, bright red in color, and milder in flavor. It is the equivalent of North India's Kashmiri chiles, which is more widely available at Indian shops. Dried Byadgi chiles are used in a variety of South Indian spice blends, along with Guntur Sannam or cayenne peppers. Use of this variety is optional but highly recommended for its unique flavor and rich red coloring.

Fresh Indian green chiles: Slender, green, and usually chopped and fried in oil or roasted whole and blended into pastes and chutneys. There are usually piles of these potent green chiles, sometimes referred to as finger chiles, in Indian shops, very difficult to miss. You can use cayenne or arbol chiles as a substitute, or even serranos or jalapeños, which are more readily available but less spicy. You can also use Thai chiles, also known as bird's eye chiles, but these have substantially more heat. To lessen the burn, remove the stems and seeds. Also note that red chiles are just ripened green chiles with a slightly different taste and similar heat levels.

Red chile powder: This powder is used primarily in pickles, batters, breads, and snack preparations. At the Indian shop, it will be labeled generically as "red chili powder." I usually look for the reddest in color because that means it is fresh, as the color of chile powder fades with time. Ground cayenne pepper can be used as a substitute, but not Mexican chili powder, which usually includes cumin, oregano, and garlic. As a garnish on yogurt raita, I will sometimes include a sprinkling of red chile powder. If you prefer less heat, paprika provides a sweeter, more mild flavor.

Fresh Ingredients

Cilantro: The herb of choice in Indian cooking, cilantro is sometimes referred to as coriander. Both the leaves and tender stems can be chopped for garnish or blended into chutneys or curry pastes. To mix it up, I like to alternate my use of cilantro with mint, parsley, dill, or basil leaves.

Curry leaves: Small, dark green leaves that give a sharp citrusy and herby flavor to dishes when fried in oil. The leaves are often confused with an ingredient in the ubiquitous, British-invented curry powder. Referred to as sweet neem, curry leaves are found in almost every South Indian dish, often paired with coconut. They are used in several ways: fried in oil, roasted and ground into spice blends or "curry powders," boiled with lentils, and pureed raw in pastes and chutneys. You will find them in fresh or dried form at Indian shops. Fresh leaves are best, but if you have access only to dry, those will work in the recipes as well but you may have to double the amount to get the full flavor. You can buy fresh curry leaves online, and if you have a green thumb, you can buy seedlings to grow at home. The seedlings fare best in a warm climate outdoors. To make the leaves last longer, you can freeze them. Before frying the fresh leaves, I rub them between my fingers to release their natural oils. Often bay leaves are noted as a substitute for curry leaves, but in my opinion curry leaves have no substitute. Always have a lid handy as you fry the leaves, as they crackle and spurt.

Ginger: A rhizome native to South India with a lemony, sharp flavor. I grew up eating primarily ginger that had been ground and added to fresh chutneys, hot pickles, and some stir-fry dishes. It's a great addition to any of the vegetable and salad dishes in the book. To quickly peel ginger, scrape the skin off with a tablespoon. Then grate it finely using a Microplane or small ginger grater. You can also freeze ginger to minimize its fibers. Thicker-skinned ginger is more pungent, while younger ginger with thinner skin is subtler in flavor.

Plain yogurt: Eaten at almost every meal in South India. It is traditional to finish a meal with yogurt mixed with plain rice for digestion. You can prepare yogurt at home (page 200).

Sweeteners and Souring Agents

Coconut: Plays an integral role in South Indian cooking and serves to add sweetness and richness to dishes. Unsweetened and grated coconut is used in most savory dishes. My first choice is, of course, grated fresh coconut, but I most often use the frozen variety that is found in the freezer aisle of Indian and Asian markets. My favorite brand is Daily Delight. When making dishes with coconut, I usually take it out of the freezer first to thaw on its own, or if I am in a rush I break a piece off and put it in the microwave on high for about fifteen seconds. You can also use the dried variety, which is often stocked in the baking aisle and more readily available in supermarkets than frozen grated coconut. In some shops, you may also find coconut flakes, which you can whizz in the food processor to become more like grated coconut or leave as is if you don't mind the large pieces. I reconstitute the dry varieties of coconut in hot water so that they plump up.

To use a fresh coconut, you will have to crack it open, peel it, and then pulse the coconut meat in a food processor or grate chunks of it. When I was growing up, my mother would crack one open with a hammer, pour out the coconut water for me to drink, and then grate the coconut using a special Indian coconut grater that consisted of a wood block and a circular blade. The frozen varieties available in Indian shops nowadays are so good that my mother and aunties are rarely seen cracking coconuts open anymore.

If none of those options suits your fancy, you can use frozen grated coconut that is sweetened. This item is quickly popping up in mainstream grocery stores. If this is what you have on hand, rinse the coconut in a fine-mesh colander to remove as much of the added sugar as possible, and then use it in the recipe. Your final option is to use coconut flour, which will not give you the substance of grated coconut but will impart the flavor and can be employed in coconut chutney or paste recipes.

Unsweetened dried coconut slices are used in some dessert and snack recipes in the book. I also use coconut milk in fruit shakes and soups.

Jaggery: One of the most unrefined sweeteners available, jaggery is used in some soups, rice dishes, and desserts. In South India, jaggery is made from the boiled-down juice of sugar cane or date palm sap. When cooled, it becomes a solid mass that is either used in chunks or ground. Its color is similar to a golden caramel. You can find jaggery in large or small chunks or in granulated form

at Indian shops. To use the solid variety, chisel off scrapings of it using a knife or pound the chunks with a hammer. I tend to have the granulated form in my kitchen as well for quick use, but you must try a taste from a solid block to understand jaggery's magic. It is sometimes referred to as medicinal sugar because it still contains many of the minerals that are stripped out from other sugars. The taste is a cross between brown sugar and molasses, but it's not as sweet as you would think. You can substitute dark brown sugar for jaggery, but its flavor lacks complexity. *Panela*, a sweetener from Latin America, or *piloncilo* from Mexico are close substitutes.

Other sweeteners: In addition to jaggery, I use granulated pure cane sugar, honey or agave nectar, and at times confectioners' sugar and demerara sugar to attain particular textures in a dessert.

Lemon: South Indian lemons are smaller and have thinner skins than the ones you may be used to. Fresh lemon juice plays a part in adding a fresh, sour flavor to many rices and vegetable stir-fries. You can substitute lime juice.

Tamarind: Fruit encased in long brown pods used as a souring agent in soups, stews, rices, and chutneys. In South Indian recipes, tamarind is often paired with coconut for a sour and sweet effect. At Indian shops, you will find tamarind blocks, pastes, and concentrates. You may also see tamarind sold in its pods. I prefer buying the block form with no stems or seeds because it is less time consuming to work with. Extracting tamarind paste is laborious, so I usually use ready-made paste. My favorite brand is Tamcon. Tamarind concentrates tend to be more watered down than pastes, so you have to add more to get the sour tang. In some instances, you can substitute lemon juice, but it lacks the sweetness of tamarind. I also purchase tamarind powder from Indian shops to add sourness to some spice blends and snack mixes.

Nuts and Seeds

Almonds: Used whole or in blanched and sliced form, mainly in dessert recipes and some beverages in the book. Blanched almonds or almond flour can also be used as a substitute for *chana dalia* or roasted *chana dal* in chutney and paste recipes. My parents each start the day by eating four almonds that have been soaked in water overnight to make their skins easy to remove. This practice is believed to improve digestion for the rest of the day.

Cashews: Primarily used to give a sweet, nutty flavor and crunchy texture to desserts and rice dishes. Raw cashew pieces are fried in ghee or butter and then added to recipes. Broken cashews are sold at Indian shops for convenient use in these recipes.

Peanuts (raw): Technically a legume, peanuts are probably the most-used "nut" in South Indian cooking. The recipes in this book typically call for raw peanuts. I prefer them with their skins on, but it is not a necessity. They are often fried in a little oil and then added to rice dishes. They are also roasted on the stove top before being skinned and added to a number of snack preparations. You can use unsalted roasted peanuts as a substitute.

Pistachios and walnuts: Used less often in South Indian cooking, but I like to use them for a different flavor and texture in desserts, rice dishes, and salads.

Seeds: My pantry is usually stocked with a wide variety of seeds, such as chia seeds, sesame seeds, flaxseed, pumpkin seeds, and sunflower seeds, which I use to garnish my sweet breakfast or dessert dishes for added texture. I'm always on the lookout for the new seed on the scene, so that list changes often.

Lentils and Beans

This group of legumes provides the bulk of the protein in the South Indian diet. By no means should you limit yourself to the ones I list here; these are just the traditional ones. In Indian shops, often lentils or split pulses—in cooked or uncooked form—is *dal*, while beans are often referred to as *gram*. If you like cooking with brown or green lentils or split peas, go right ahead and adapt the recipes in the book for them. The texture will be different, but you will no doubt get a tasty dish out of it. The first name you see for these entries is how you will most likely find these labeled at the market. Sometimes this is a common English term, like lentil, and other times it isn't, like dal. In the parentheses are common alternative terms or descriptors. In the recipes, the first term will be used.

Chana dal, without skin (split black chickpeas): Similar in appearance to split yellow peas (and often mislabeled as such), but larger in size and with a slightly wrinkled surface. A quick way to tell that you have chana dal rather than split yellow peas is that a few in the bag usually still have some of their brown skin. Chana dal is the skinned and split version of black chickpeas. Chana dal, like urud dal, is fried in oil and used to give a nutty and crunchy texture to dishes. If it is not fried long enough, it is too hard to eat; one trick to safeguard against that is to soak it in hot water for ten to fifteen minutes before frying. You can also use soaked chana dal as a substitute for roasted chana dal in recipes for pastes or chutneys. After soaking this dal, you can also throw it into salads like *kosambri* (page 61) or grind it to make steamed cakes (page 48).

Roasted chana dal, without skin (chana dalia): Used primarily as a thickening agent for South Indian chutneys and curries, roasted chana dal is off-white in color. It is sometimes referred to as chana dalia, not to be confused with whole roasted chana or roasted chana dal that still has its brown skin, which is also available in Indian shops. I usually powder this ingredient before grinding it with coconut, chiles, and herbs to make a spice paste or chutney. In some Indian shops, you may also find preground roasted chana dal. As a substitute, you can soak chana dal in hot water for fifteen minutes or use blanched almonds or almond flour, but the flavor of the recipe will be altered slightly.

Mung beans (whole moong): A small green and protein-rich bean that can be sprouted for use in salads. I like to soak and grind them into batter for making a quick and unfermented *dosa* (page 43), or savory crepe. Native to India and sometimes referred to as mung beans, the Indian variety of the bean is smaller than the one used for Chinese mung bean sprouts and takes less time to germinate and sprout, about a day versus three days.

Moong dal (split mung beans without skin): Yellow lentils are made into thick soups or soaked and used in salads and stir-fry dishes. Not to be confused with split yellow peas, moong dal is smaller in size and is the split and skinned version of mung beans or whole moong. For the recipes in this book, make sure not to pick up the variety that still has its green skin intact.

Red lentils (masoor dal): Red lentils are more easily found at the grocery store and cook more quickly than the more traditional toor dal. In fact, nowadays many of my aunts prefer this lentil over toor dal for this reason. It can be used in place of toor dal in all of the recipes in the book.

Toor dal (split pigeon peas): Indigenous to India and prepared throughout the country, toor dal is the most commonly used lentil in everyday South Indian cooking. My parents prepare this earthy and full-flavored golden lentil more often than any other type. In Indian shops, you can purchase an oily or nonoily toor dal. The oil is used to preserve the dal for a longer time. There is no difference in cooking times, but if you buy the oily type you must wash it very well. I buy the nonoily version, as the type of oil used is usually not listed on the package. Red lentils can be substituted for toor dal.

Urad whole gota (black gram without skin): These round, white beans are the whole form of urad dal with the skins removed and are used primarily to make a steamed cake called idli and a savory crepe called dosa. The bean is sometimes referred to as black gram. In Indian shops, you will also find whole urad dal with the black skins intact. You can use this variety as well; it will just put black flecks into your dosa or idli batter. If you can't find the whole variety, you can make dosas and idlis with split urad dal, preferably skinned.

Urad dal (split black gram without skin): Although the skinned beans are white in color, in its original form urad dal has a black skin. Indian shops also carry varieties

of split urad dal with the black skin still on, so make sure to get the skinned variety. In South India, this dal functions as a spice and is fried in oil to give a nutty and crunchy texture to rice and vegetable stir-fries or to season chutneys. This lentil is sometimes referred to as split black gram or split matpe beans.

The following beans and legumes are mentioned peripherally in the book, but they are on permanent rotation in my kitchen. I often reach for these in the winter months when seasonal local vegetables are in scant supply.

Black-eyed peas: These are often available in dried, frozen, or canned form. These beans are often cooked with lentils and usually paired with greens or eggplant (page 137).

Kala chana (black chickpeas): These chickpeas are similar to regular chickpeas but slightly smaller and with dark brown skin. These are sometimes referred to as desi chickpea or black Bengal gram. You can cook them or sprout them just like a chickpea; they just take longer to cook. Their skinned and split form is used more often and is referred to as chana dal (page 28). Besan, Indian chickpea flour (page 32), is made from this variety of chickpea.

Horse gram (kulthi bean, brown lentils): Like black chickpeas, these beans can be cooked or sprouted for use in soups or salads, and they take time to cook. Their advantage is that they are one of the healthiest legumes, packed with protein and calcium.

Spice Blends

South Indian kitchens contain a number of spice blends that are frequently used to flavor a wide variety of dishes. The most prominent are saaru or rasam powder and huli or sambar powder. I have provided spice blend recipes on pages 194 to 199 so you can make your own, and they are also readily available at the Indian shop or online.

Rice and Grains

South Indian food revolves around white rice as its main grain, but I love to mix it up with alternatives such as brown rice, couscous, quinoa, sorghum, farro, kamut, bulgur, wheat berries, freekeh, millet, barley, and buckwheat groats. Lately, I've also gotten into alternative noodles, such as bean thread and sweet potato, that I find at the Asian market. If you also tend to cook with a range of grains, I recommend substituting them for rice in the recipes in this book for a bit of variety.

Rice: Numerous varieties of rice are grown in South India, from short grain to long grain. In my household, I alternate between using steamed Dehraduni basmati rice, which is what I grew up eating, and a South Indian variety of medium-grain rice called *sona masuri*, which is available in Indian shops. A North Indian variety with a strong fragrance, basmati is not traditionally used in making South Indian dishes, but I enjoy its long grains that stay separate when cooked. In fact, my grandmother would often make *sanna akki*, a type of rice with shorter and thicker grains, which was stickier and more beneficial for soaking up brothy soups and stews when eaten with the hand. I leave rice preference up to you, but basmati, sona masuri, or jasmine rice will work just fine for the recipes in this book. I use long-grain for making dosas and savory crepes, and short-grain rice for making batter for idlis, or steamed rice cakes. Idli rice is sold in Indian shops; parboiled or short-grain rice varieties like Arborio can be substituted.

Shavige: Vermicelli or thin noodles made from rice or semolina and typically used in desserts or stir-fry dishes. At Indian shops, you can purchase the dried noodles or ones that are preroasted and cut into bite-size pieces. The noodles are roasted beforehand so they do not stick together while cooking. You can substitute Asian-style rice noodles or angel hair pasta.

Flours

These are the flours used in recipes in this book, but I also list alternative flour options within recipes.

Atta: Finely ground whole-wheat durum flour used to make Indian breads such as chapati and *poori*. Cultivated in India for centuries, *atta* is a low-gluten flour, perfect for making elastic doughs that can be rolled thin. For a substitute you can use white whole-wheat flour or one part whole-wheat and one part all-purpose flour.

Besan or gram flour (Indian chickpea flour): A gluten-free and high-protein flour milled from chana dal, or split black chickpeas. Although sometimes referred to as chickpea flour, the consistency of besan is not as soft as flour made from white chickpeas or garbanzo beans, but as a last resort you can use it as a substitute, or use all-purpose flour. Besan is used mostly for making batters for fried appetizers such as *bhajji* (page 148), *pakoda*, and *bonda* and in some sweets.

Rice flour: Finely milled gluten-free flour made from rice. I add it to batters to improve crispness. You can substitute brown rice flour for white.

Sooji or rava (Indian semolina flour): This type of semolina flour is made from soft wheat and is whiter in color than Italian semolina, which is made from hard durum wheat and is yellow in color. Indian semolina flour is sometimes referred to as farina or by the brand name Cream of Wheat in its finely ground form, both of which are easily found in most supermarkets. You will find a variety of different textures of semolina sold in Indian shops. I usually buy the medium-coarse or coarse variety to make rava idli, or steamed dumplings (page 50). In India, the finer varieties of the flour are used to make desserts like kadabu (page 163) and some fried snacks. I use polenta or cornmeal as a substitute for sooji in some traditional dishes like *upma*, a breakfast porridge (page 55).

Cooking Oils and Ghee

When cooking the majority of the recipes in this book, I generally use mild-flavored oils with high smoke points such as sunflower, safflower, grapeseed, peanut (untoasted), or organic canola. Traditionally, my grandmother would use peanut oil for the majority of her recipes. For some recipes I use coconut oil when I want an extra boost of coconut flavor. I never use extra-virgin olive oil when cooking Indian dishes because of its strong flavor. Also, on account of its low smoke point, I find that black mustard seeds, which are used in most every recipe in the book, do not pop as well in olive oil.

Ghee, or *thuppa* in Kannada, is Indian-style clarified butter made from boiling butter until it becomes clear and browned milk solids settle to the bottom. These milk solids, which give the butter its distinctive, nutty flavor, are then separated out. The resulting cooking fat is rich and flavorful and makes your house smell like heaven when you fry anything in it. It has a higher smoke point than butter and most oils. Since it contains no milk, it can be kept at room temperature for 2 weeks and in the refrigerator for a few months. Ghee has been used in ayurveda for centuries as a healthful ingredient and also plays a part in some Hindu rituals. You can make ghee at home (page 202) or buy it at Indian shops and some specialty markets. For a substitute you can use unsalted butter.

Salt

I use fine-grain sea salt or Diamond Crystal brand kosher salt the majority of the time, and fleur de sel or any flaky sea salt I have collected along the way as a finishing salt for some dishes. If you use Morton brand kosher salt or any variety of table salt, proceed with caution, as these salts tend to be more potent.

Kitchen Tools

Here is a list of specialized pieces of kitchen equipment, which can be purchased at the Indian shop or online (see the resources on page 206). The items are listed according to how often I use them in the kitchen.

Tempering pot: A little heavy-bottomed, bowl-shaped pot with a long handle used to fry whole spices like black mustard seeds and cumin seeds in hot oil or ghee. This hot mixture is then poured over different dishes as a final seasoning. You can use a small frying pan or even a Turkish coffee pot instead. Here's a little secret: I also use my Indian tempering pot to poach eggs because it's the perfect size to keep the egg intact.

Masala dabba or spice tiffin: A traditional stainless steel Indian spice box (photo below) usually containing seven small spice containers, an inner cover, and a spice spoon. Every Indian kitchen has one, or two in my case. I have one with my main South Indian spices and one with my North Indian spices. I use the inner cover to hold a small stash of dried red chiles. A spice tiffin is not necessary but can be a time saver, because you can fit your most-used spices into one canister, instead of fumbling with multiple bottles.

Idli stand: Stainless steel molds used to make idlis (photo page 46), steamed lentil and rice cakes that resemble flying saucers. I also use these molds to make

steamed lentil and herb dumplings called *nuchinunde* (page 50). I have provided a DIY alternative using a pie pan, but the stand is an inexpensive purchase at an Indian shop or online.

Powerful blender: One of the most important tools in an Indian kitchen, a blender is used for making spice pastes, chutneys, dosa and idli batters, vegetable purees, and shakes. For making the spice pastes and chutneys in this book, a strong blender with a small container, like a Magic Bullet, is very effective because some recipes involve first pulverizing dals and spices and then grinding coconut and herbs. The preferred equipment for making dosa and idli batters is an Indian wet grinder, which does not require much water and is able to pulverize the dal optimally, but a Vitamix with a large container does the trick for me, because it aerates the batter effectively. I also use my Vitamix for grinding roasted spices for all of my bulk spice blends. I don't want to imply that you must go out and buy a Magic Bullet or Vitamix, because truth be told, my mother has been making all of the recipes in this book for decades using a standard blender. It just makes things easier. I also use an immersion blender to puree cooked lentils into paste for some recipes.

Stainless steel coffee filter: A two-chambered vessel used for making South Indian filter coffee. You can also use a French press.

CHAPATI TOOLS

Chapati or roti (page 115) are traditional North Indian flatbreads that are not served as often as rice in South Indian homes, but they do make an appearance from time to time. I have included my father's recipe for chapatis in the book, and if you decide you'd like to make these on a regular basis, the following tools will make the job easier:

Tava: A concave heavy iron skillet used to cook chapatis or North Indian roti. You can substitute a cast-iron frying pan or griddle. I have a specific tava that I have designated for making only Indian roti recipes or for warming corn tortillas, which I generally don't add any oil to.

Bellan: A small Indian rolling pin used for rolling chapatis and dough. You can use a small rolling pin instead.

Chakla: A round wooden board with pegs on the bottom, used for rolling out chapatis and dough. You can just as easily use a clean counter, but a chakla requires less cleanup.

Chimta: Flat metal tongs used for cooking chapatis on an open flame.

1

BREAKFAST AND LIGHT MEALS

Indian breakfast for the most part is savory and oftentimes spicy in nature. South Indian breakfasts are no exception to that rule. The dishes in this chapter are served interchangeably for breakfast or as a snack. You will find many of them in starring roles on menus at local eateries in Bangalore, where people order them at all times of the day. One of the most famous of these dishes is masala dosa (page 42), a savory crepe filled with potato curry and served with spicy coconut chutney.

Weekends were when my mother shared a breadth of the breakfast foods she grew up eating in Bangalore. The dishes ranged from rice and lentil cakes called idlis (page 48) to a savory semolina and vegetable porridge called uppittu (page 55). I remember waking up on Saturday and Sunday mornings to first a clatter of pots (maybe my mother's way of waking us up) and then the aroma of spices frying in the kitchen. Some of my fondest memories growing up are of eating one of my mother's specialties, her homemade yogurt and spicy chutney pudi (page 190), in front of my Saturday morning cartoons.

RICE AND LENTIL CREPE *Dosa*

Ⓥ Ⓖ All seasons • Serves 6 to 8; makes about 18 crepes

VIBRANT INDIA

Dosa, a crepe made from a fermented batter of rice and lentils, is one of the most popular foods in South India. Ask any Bangalorean and they'll name their favorite place to eat dosa and expound on why their choice is the best. In a South Indian restaurant, you may find yourself face to face with one of these gigantic crispy crepes, which is very different from dosas made in the home. The dosas I grew up eating were soft with a crunchy surface and were usually the size of a plate. My favorite ways to eat dosas are with one of my mom's coconut chutneys and homemade yogurt or with the works, like the masala dosa on page 42.

The warm climate of South India is optimal for fermenting dosa batter. In my colder New York apartment, I use my oven light and a large bowl of hot water to help it along. The simplest dosa recipe consists of just rice, lentils, water, and salt. It takes a couple days to make, as you must soak and grind ingredients and then ferment the batter overnight.

I add cooked rice for a little extra crispness, fenugreek seeds for fluffiness and to help aid in fermentation, and chana dal for a nice golden color and also for crispness. In this recipe, you can use urad whole gota or its split form, urad dal, preferably without skin.

2 cups uncooked long-grain or basmati rice

Filtered water

½ cup urad whole gota or urad dal, preferably without skin

2 tablespoons chana dal

1 teaspoon fenugreek seeds

¼ cup cooked rice

1½ teaspoons kosher salt (not iodized)

Ghee (page 202) or mild-flavored oil such as canola, for frying

SERVING OPTIONS

Chutney (pages 179 to 183)

Huli (page 131 to 138)

Potato curry (page 80)

Plain yogurt

Chutney pudi (page 190)

Making Dosa Batter

Wash the uncooked rice and place it in a bowl. Add enough filtered water to cover the rice by 2 inches. (Filtered water is important in case there is a high amount of chlorine in your water, which will inhibit fermentation.) Rinse the urad whole gota and chana dal and place in a separate bowl with the fenugreek seeds. (Good-quality urad will give off some bubbles when rinsed in water.) Add enough filtered water to cover the urad by 2 inches.

Soak both mixtures, uncovered, for at least 6 hours or up to overnight. I usually put the bowls near my houseplants, as wild yeast from the plants helps to ferment the batter.

If you don't have leftover rice, make some to include in the batter the next day. This ingredient adds crispyness but is not mandatory.

continued

The next morning, drain the urad and fenugreek, saving the soaking liquid. Place the urad mixture in a blender (an Indian wet grinder is best, but a powerful blender also works well). With the machine running, slowly add about 1 cup of the reserved soaking liquid to the container, until you get a smooth, light, and fluffy batter. You may have to grind the urad in batches, depending on the size and strength of your blender. Do not let the batter overheat. To check that your urad has been ground finely enough, drop a little into a bowl of water. If it rises to the top, it has been ground enough. Pour the batter into a large mixing bowl.

Repeat the same process for the rice, in batches if necessary, using about 1 cup of the reserved soaking liquid. Once the soaked rice is ground, add the cooked rice and grind further. The batter will be smooth but will feel slightly grainy to the touch.

Pour the rice batter into the mixing bowl with the ground urad mixture, and add the salt. Mix the ground rice and urad together with your hand. The heat in your hand is good to kick-start the fermentation process while also adding more wild yeast. You should have a loose, thick batter that falls through your fingers easily but also coats your hands.

Cover the bowl with a tea towel and set it in a warm place. The batter needs to be at a temperature of 80° to 90°F to ferment. (I usually place my batter in the oven with the light on and a large bowl of hot tap water below it. I change

out the water a few times to keep the oven warm and humid. Home cooks in cold climates use many different methods, from placing the bowl on a heating pad to wrapping it in a blanket.) Depending on the temperature, your batter could take 8 to 20 hours to ferment. When fermented, it will have almost doubled and will look puffed up on the top. It will also have a sour, fermented smell. When you scoop it with a spoon, it will be a frothy mass of bubbles. Note that in colder climates, your batter may not rise as much, but if it has a frothy, bubbly look and smells fermented, you can start making dosas with it.

Cooking a Dosa

Stir the batter a couple of times. Ideally, you have a thick, flowing batter; it's thicker than crepe batter. If too thick, add filtered water little by little.

Before cooking the dosas, set a little bowl with ghee and a teaspoon, a metal spatula, a cup of water, and a few paper towels or a silicone pastry brush by the stove. I use a ⅓-cup measure to scoop up the batter and a large, slightly curved serving spoon to spread it in the skillet.

Put a well-seasoned cast-iron skillet* over medium heat. Put a couple of drops of ghee in the skillet and lightly smear it all over using a paper towel or silicone pastry brush. A technique that restaurants use is to stick a fork in the top of a cut onion and put the cut side down on the skillet to smear the oil. This step helps to make the surface of the skillet more nonstick. At this point, you don't want to add too much oil, as this will make it difficult to spread the dosa evenly. Sprinkle a few drops of water on the skillet to check whether it's hot. If the water sizzles, it's time. Turn the heat to low.

Scoop up ⅓ cup of batter, using your measuring cup, and pour it into the center of the skillet.** The batter should sizzle a bit when it hits the skillet. Starting in the middle, swirl the batter outward in a circular motion, using the bottom of a large, slightly curved serving spoon, a flat ladle, or the measuring cup, until you have spread it out into a round dosa that is about 9 inches in diameter. It is important not to press down too hard with your spreading utensil. The reason a slightly curved or flat utensil is best is that if the bottom has too much contact with the skillet it will become hot and make it difficult for you to spread the batter. Spreading should happen more on the top surface than on the bottom.

When you've finished spreading the dosa batter, turn the heat back up to medium. Wait a few seconds for the dosa to sizzle a little in the pan, and then drip about 1 teaspoon of melted ghee around the edges of the dosa and on top. If you have an oil sprayer, that will do the job efficiently. Cook until the dosa is dried out on top and you can see some browning and crisp spots appearing on the bottom, 2 to 3 minutes. When it's ready, the dosa will peel off easily when you slide your spatula underneath. If you see the dosa browning but it

is still sticking, just lower the heat and wait a few seconds. Then probe around the edges with your spatula until you find an area that starts to give, and usually the whole dosa will unstick once you start to pull it up from that spot. Flip your dosa over for a few seconds and then flip it over again. Fold the dosa in half in the skillet and slide it onto a plate for serving.

You must cool down your skillet so you can easily spread your next dosa and prevent it from sticking to the pan. To cool it down, sprinkle a little water on its surface. When the sizzling stops, heat the skillet back up for your next dosa. Stir the dosa batter well before scooping up batter for the next one.

Serve as a masala dosa with chutney, huli, and curry, or with yogurt and chutney pudi.

You can refrigerate leftover batter; it will keep for about a week. If you do this, bring your batter back to room temperature before making the dosas. This will ensure that your dosas have a nice golden color when cooked. I personally prefer to make dosas right after the batter has fermented, as it results in the best texture and color.

---

*If using a nonstick skillet, you can reduce the amount of oil used to cook the dosa.

**To make a paper dosa, which is thinner and crunchier, you can use ¼ cup of batter and spread it thinner in the skillet. For extra crispiness, use your spatula to flatten the batter down once you have spread it.

continued

Dosa Variations

POTATO-FILLED CREPE *Masala Dosa*

Masala dosa is the king of dosas; a mouthwatering one. It's filled with buttery and bright yellow potato curry (page 80) and served with coconut chutney (page 179 to 181) and mixed vegetable huli (page 131) or sambar. In Bangalore there are numerous landmark eateries serving up the most delicious homestyle masala dosas. At Vidyarthi Bhavan, a Brahmin-style café in the city, barefoot waiters wearing crisp blue uniforms and bleached white *dhotis* (long loincloths) carry impressive stacks of their specialty, benne "butter" masala dosas. I crave these often.

RICE, LENTIL, AND VEGETABLE PANCAKE *Uttapam*

Uttapam is a savory pancake made with leftover dosa batter (page 38). Usually, dosa batter is thicker the day after it's made, so it's perfect for making uttapam. The pancake is porous, has a bit of crispness on the outside, and is soft and pillowy on the inside. It's sometimes referred to as the South Indian pizza and is usually cooked with finely chopped onion, tomatoes, green chiles, and cilantro. To make uttapam, spoon dosa batter into the middle of a hot, lightly oiled skillet, just like a pancake, top it with your choice of fresh vegetables, and cook on both sides. Serve with chutney (pages 179 to 183).

MUNG BEAN AND QUINOA CREPE *Pesarattu*

(V) (G) All seasons • Serves 4 to 6, makes about 14 crepes

In South India, there is never a lack of ingredients for making dosas. Home cooks will take any mixture of soaked lentils or beans and rice or grains to make delicious crepes that are not always fermented. Many times, a mix of onion, coconut, cilantro, chiles, and spices will also be added to these batters.

This dosa is my riff on pesarattu, a soft mung bean dosa. Since pesarattu is unfermented, you just soak the ingredients the day before and then blend and make your dosa the next day. I've added quinoa to my batter for more protein.

I hope this recipe will give you some ideas to get creative with savory crepes in your kitchen using different grains, seeds, lentils, and beans. Another example of an unfermented dosa is my adai recipe on page 44, made from soaked lentils and steel-cut oats.

If you love cheese, as I do, you may even fill your dosa with sharp Cheddar, along with chutney, for a tasty quesadilla.

1 cup mung beans

½ cup quinoa

½ teaspoon fenugreek seeds

1 small yellow onion, quartered

½-inch piece fresh ginger, peeled

3 or 4 Indian green chiles or serrano chiles, or a few dried red chiles

10 mint leaves or 2 tablespoons cilantro leaves

1 teaspoon cumin seeds

⅛ teaspoon asafetida (hing) powder

About 1 teaspoon salt

Ghee (page 202) or mild-flavored oil such as canola, for frying

SERVING OPTIONS

Chutney (pages 179 to 183)

Huli (pages 131 to 137)

Potato curry (page 80)

Plain yogurt

Chutney pudi (page 190)

Rinse the mung beans and quinoa and place in a bowl. Add the fenugreek seeds and cover with water by about 2 inches. Soak overnight.

The next day, drain the soaked mixture, discarding the soaking liquid. Place the soaked mixture in a blender. With the machine running, add water, a little at a time, until you are able to grind the mixture into a paste. It will take about 2 cups of water. Add the onion, ginger, chiles, mint leaves, cumin seeds, asafetida, and salt to the blender and blend until you have a smooth, thick, pourable batter.

Follow the directions for cooking a dosa on page 40, using ¼ cup of batter for each 8-inch crepe.

Serve with chutney, huli, and curry, or with yogurt and chutney pudi.

BREAKFAST AND LIGHT MEALS

MIXED LENTIL AND OATMEAL CREPE *Adai*

Ⓥ Ⓖ All seasons • Serves 6 to 8, makes about 18 crepes

Like pesarattu (page 43), adai is an unfermented dosa prepared in South Indian homes. This savory crepe is made from soaked rice, lentils, and red chiles ground together with coconut, onion, herbs, and spices. For my version, I use steel-cut oats, four types of lentils, and leeks. The recipe is quite forgiving, so you can use different varieties of rice or lentils that you have on hand. I sometimes make this crepe with brown rice instead of oats, which results in a crunchier crepe.

Adai is often served with avial (page 94), but don't let that stop you from pairing the flavorful crepe with your heart's desire. On weekends, I will sometimes make adai dosa breakfast wraps filled with sautéed seasonal vegetables, hard-boiled egg, and my go-to dressing of hummus, plain yogurt, and Brooklyn Delhi achaar.

1¼ cups steel-cut oats or brown or white rice

4 or 5 dried red chiles

¼ cup chana dal or yellow split peas

¼ cup toor dal or red lentils

¼ cup moong dal

¼ cup urad dal

½ cup unsweetened grated coconut (fresh, frozen, or dried)

2 leeks or 1 medium yellow onion, coarsely chopped

½-inch piece fresh ginger, peeled

1 sprig curry leaves (about 20 leaves)

¼ cup cilantro leaves

¼ teaspoon asafetida (hing) powder

¼ teaspoon turmeric powder

1½ teaspoons salt

¼ teaspoon freshly ground black pepper

Ghee (page 202) or mild-flavored oil such as canola, for frying

SERVING OPTIONS

Chutney (pages 179 to 183)

Huli (pages 131 to 138)

Potato curry (page 80)

Plain yogurt

Chutney pudi (page 190)

Place the steel-cut oats in a bowl with the dried chiles, and add water to cover by 2 inches. Rinse the dals in a fine-mesh sieve. Place the dals in a separate bowl and add water to cover by 2 inches.

Soak both mixtures for at least 4 hours or up to overnight.

Thaw frozen coconut or place dried coconut in a little hot water to plump it up. Drain both soaked mixtures, discarding the soaking liquid, and place in a blender with the leeks, coconut, ginger, curry leaves, cilantro leaves, asafetida, turmeric, salt, and pepper. Puree with enough water, about 2 cups, to result in a thick but pourable batter.

Follow the directions for cooking a dosa on page 40, using ¼ cup of batter for each 8-inch crepe.

Serve with chutney, huli, and curry, or with yogurt and chutney pudi.

STEAMED SEMOLINA CAKES *Rava Idli*

 All seasons • Serves 2 or 3; makes 12 small idlis

Rava idlis are the instant version of traditional idlis (page 48), in that they are not fermented. They are made with a batter of Indian semolina flour and yogurt and flavored with ginger, herbs, fried spices, and cashews.

Mahvelli Tiffin Rooms (MTR), the famous restaurant chain in Bangalore specializing in South Indian–style classics like dosa and idli, claims to have invented this recipe. During World War II, when there was a shortage of rice for making idlis, MTR created the rava idli, using semolina as a substitute. The MTR mix is readily available in Indian stores, but this recipe comes from my Auntie Latha in Bangalore.

Traditionally, idlis were steamed in banana or jackfruit leaves, but now they are most often made using an idli stand (photo page 46), which you can purchase for a modest price at an Indian shop. If you want to DIY, though, I have a trick using a pie pan and a steamer basket. There's actually a similarly shaped idli made on a plate called kanchipuram idli or thatte idli, so you're not too off base steaming them in this fashion.

You can make this batter the night before for steaming the next morning.

¼ teaspoon ghee (page 202) or unsalted butter

2 tablespoons raw cashews, broken or chopped into large pieces

1 tablespoon mild-flavored oil such as canola

¼ teaspoon black mustard seeds

½ teaspoon cumin seeds

½ teaspoon chana dal

½ teaspoon urad dal

4 or 5 fresh curry leaves, coarsely chopped

½-inch piece fresh ginger, peeled and grated

2 Indian green chiles or serrano chiles

1 cup coarse Indian semolina (sooji, rava) or farina

1 cup plain whole-milk yogurt, lightly beaten by hand

2 tablespoons chopped cilantro leaves

¾ teaspoon salt

¼ teaspoon baking soda

SERVING OPTIONS

Chutney (pages 179 to 183)

Chutney pudi (page 190)

Plain yogurt

Karnataka coconut vegetable curry (page 95)

Put the ghee in a wok or sauté pan over medium heat. When melted, add the cashew pieces and fry until they start to turn golden brown and fragrant, about 2 minutes. Set aside in a bowl lined with a paper towel.

Put the oil in the same wok or sauté pan over medium heat. When the oil is hot and shimmering, add one black mustard seed. When the seed sizzles and pops, add the rest of the mustard seeds. Keep a lid handy to cover the pan while the mustard seeds are popping. When the popping starts to subside (a few seconds), immediately add the cumin seeds, chana dal, and urad dal. Stir to coat with oil, and turn the heat down to medium-low.

continued

Continue to stir the dals so they roast evenly, until they turn a reddish golden brown and smell nutty, less than a minute. Rub the curry leaves between your fingers a little to release their natural oils, and drop them, the ginger, and green chiles into the oil. Cover immediately, as moisture from the curry leaves will cause the oil to spatter. Then stir to evenly coat everything with oil and continue to fry until the ginger and chiles are less raw, 10 to 15 seconds.

Mix in the semolina and roasted cashews and turn off the heat. Place the mixture on a plate to cool.

When cooled, combine the semolina mixture with the beaten yogurt, chopped cilantro, salt, and baking soda in a medium bowl. Mix until there are no lumps. Set aside for 5 minutes.

If using an idli stand, add water to a stockpot or large pot, making sure the water level is below the last rung of the idli stand. Bring the water to a boil. Disassemble the idli stand. Put a drop of oil in each idli mold, and smear it all over the mold with your hand or a paper towel.

Check your batter for consistency. When placed in the molds, it should not be stiff and lumpy; it should be a thick batter that settles into place. I usually add about 1½ tablespoons of water to get it to this point.

Fill the molds with the batter. Stack the levels (there are usually three) back into the idli stand and secure them. Make sure to stagger the plates so that idlis are not directly below the ones on the level above.

If using a pie pan, place a steamer basket at the bottom of a pot, with water below it. Bring the water to a boil. Lightly oil the pie pan and then fill it about ½ inch deep with idli batter.

Place the idli stand or pie plate in the pot. Cover and steam over medium heat until the idlis are cooked through, 10 to 12 minutes. Turn off the heat. Lift the idli stand or pie plate out of the pot and let cool for 2 minutes.

Using a wet spoon, remove the idlis from the idli stand. If the first idli is not smooth on the bottom when taken out, the idlis need to cool a bit longer. If you used a pie pan, cut the idli into equal wedges with a knife.

Serve immediately with chutney and yogurt or Karnataka coconut vegetable curry.

STEAMED RICE AND LENTIL CAKES *Idli*

 All seasons • Serves 6 to 8; makes about 24 idlis

Idli is dosa's healthier cousin. Like a dosa, it's made from a fermented batter of rice and urad and takes a couple days to prepare, but instead of being cooked in a skillet, it is steamed into soft dumplings resembling flying saucers. They are usually soaked in huli and doused with coconut chutney. You can also just eat them with plain yogurt or butter and a sprinkling of chutney pudi. In this recipe, you can use urad whole gota or its split form, urad dal, preferably without skin. Similar to the recipe for idli rava on page 45, you can steam this batter in a traditional idli pan or in a pie pan.

2 cups uncooked idli rice or parboiled rice or short-grain rice such as Arborio

Filtered water

1 cup urad whole gota or urad dal, preferably without skin

½ teaspoon fenugreek seeds (optional)

¼ cup cooked rice

1½ teaspoons kosher salt (not iodized)

SERVING OPTIONS

Huli (pages 131 to 137)

Chutney (pages 179 to 183)

Chutney pudi (page 190)

Plain yogurt

Butter

Wash the uncooked rice and place it in a bowl. Add enough filtered water to cover the rice by 2 inches. (Filtered water is important because too much chlorine will inhibit fermentation.) Rinse the whole urad gota and place in a separate bowl with the fenugreek seeds. (Good-quality urad will give off some bubbles when rinsed in water.) Add enough filtered water to cover the urad by 2 inches.

Soak both mixtures, uncovered, for at least 6 hours or up to overnight. I usually put the bowls near my houseplants, as wild yeast from the plants helps to ferment the batter. (The more wild yeast you can get to attach itself to the soaking urad, the better. Fenugreek in particular is good at attracting wild yeast in the air.)

If you don't have leftover rice, make some to include in the batter the next day.

The next morning, drain the urad mixture, saving the soaking liquid. Place the mixture in a blender (an Indian wet grinder is best, but a powerful blender also works well). With the machine running, slowly add 1 to 1¼ cups of the reserved soaking liquid, until you get a smooth, light, and fluffy batter. You may have to blend in batches, depending on the size and strength of your blender. Do not let the batter overheat. To check that your urad has been ground finely enough, drop a little into a bowl of water. If it rises to the top, it has been ground enough. Pour the batter into a large mixing bowl.

VIBRANT INDIA

Repeat the same process for the rice, in batches if necessary, using ¾ to 1 cup of the reserved soaking liquid. Once the soaked rice is ground, add the cooked rice and grind further. The batter will be smooth but will feel slightly grainy to the touch.

Pour the rice batter into the mixing bowl with the ground urad mixture and add the salt. Mix the blended rice and urad together with your hand. You should have a loose, thick batter that falls through your fingers but also coats your hands.

Cover the bowl with a tea towel and set it in a warm place. The batter needs to be at a temperature of 80° to 90°F to ferment. (I usually place my batter in the oven with the light on and a large bowl of hot tap water below it. I change out the water a few times to keep the oven warm and humid.) Depending on the conditions, your batter could take 8 to 20 hours to ferment. When fermented, it will have almost doubled and will look puffed up on the top. It will also have a sour, fermented smell. When you scoop it with a spoon, it will be a frothy mass of bubbles. Note that in colder climates, your batter may not rise as much.

I try not to stir my idli batter at this point, because I find it makes softer, more airy idlis if used as is. Your batter should be thick and fluffy but still pourable. Add water if needed.

If using an idli stand, add water to a stockpot or large pot, making sure the water level is below the last rung of the idli stand. Bring the water to a boil. Disassemble the idli stand. Put a drop of oil in each idli mold, smear it all over the mold with your hand or a paper towel.

Fill the molds with the batter. Stack the levels (there are usually three) back into the idli stand and secure them. Stagger the plates so that idlis are not directly below the ones on the level above.

To use a pie pan, place a steamer basket at the bottom of a pot, with water below it. Bring the water to a boil. Lightly oil the pie pan and then fill it about ½ inch deep with idli batter.

Place the idli stand or pie pan in the pot. Cover and steam over medium heat until the idlis are cooked through, about 10 minutes. Turn off the heat. Lift the idli stand or pie pan out of the pot and let cool for 2 minutes.

Using a wet spoon, remove the idlis from the idli stand. If the first idli is not smooth on the bottom when taken out, the idlis need to cool a bit longer. If you used a pie pan, cut the idli into equal wedges with a knife.

Serve the idlis with huli, chutney, and a dollop of yogurt on top, or plain with butter. Idlis are best served hot. If you do need to reheat them, sprinkle them with water, cover with a paper towel, and microwave briefly to resteam them.

You can refrigerate leftover batter; it will keep for about a week. If you do this, bring your batter back to room temperature before making the idlis. I prefer to make idlis right after the batter has fermented, as it results in the softest, most airy idlis.

STEAMED LENTIL AND HERB DUMPLINGS *Nuchinunde*

Ⓥ Ⓖ All seasons • Serves 4; makes about 30 dumplings

Nuchinunde are steamed lentil and herb dumplings made with toor dal (split pigeon peas) and sometimes a mix of other lentils as well. They are a specialty of Mysore and are rarely found on restaurant menus. This recipe is adapted from my Auntie Asha, who made them for me the first time I had them. She also includes moong dal and chana dal in her nuchinunde. The moong dal is used to help bind the dough and also for digestion.

I use dill and cilantro in this recipe, but feel free to substitute different combinations of herbs, such as curry leaves and mint or even chopped spinach. The dumplings go best with a quick yogurt sauce. The batter will keep in the refrigerator for a couple of days, so you can make it and have fresh dumplings quickly. You can steam the dumplings in lightly greased idli molds or a pie pan.

½ cup toor dal

¼ cup moong dal

2 tablespoons chana dal

¼ cup unsweetened grated coconut (fresh, frozen, or dried)

1 teaspoon peeled, grated fresh ginger

4 or 5 Indian green chiles or serrano chiles, finely chopped

¼ teaspoon asafetida (hing) powder

1 teaspoon salt

½ teaspoon cumin seeds

About ½ cup finely chopped yellow onion

¼ cup finely chopped dill or mint leaves

½ cup finely chopped cilantro leaves

SERVING OPTIONS

Quick yogurt sauce (page 71) or raita (pages 72 to 76)

Plain yogurt

Cilantro coconut chutney (page 179)

Wash all the dals thoroughly, using a fine-mesh colander. Cover the dals with water by at least 2 inches and soak for 4 hours. Thaw frozen coconut or place dried coconut in hot water to plump.

Drain the dals and grind them with the ginger and green chiles in a food processor. It's okay if there are still some whole pieces of dal in there. Transfer to a mixing bowl. Stir in the asafetida, salt, cumin seeds, coconut, onion, dill, and cilantro.

Take a heaping tablespoon of the batter and, using your hands, form it into a 2-inch oblong. Repeat with the rest of the dough to get about 30 pieces.

If using an idli stand, add water to a stockpot or soup pot, making sure the water level is below the last rung of the idli stand. Bring the water to a boil. Disassemble the idli stand. Lightly grease each idli mold and place a dumpling in each indentation. Stack the levels (there are usually three) back into the idli stand and secure them. Make sure to stagger the plates so that dumplings are not directly below the ones on the level above.

If using a pie pan, place a steamer basket at the bottom of a pot, with water below it. Bring the water to a boil. Lightly oil the pie pan and place the dumplings in the pan.

Place the idli stand or pie pan in the pot. Cover and steam over medium-high heat until the nuchinunde are cooked through, 12 to 14 minutes. Turn off the heat.

Serve hot with yogurt sauce or yogurt and chutney.

VERMICELLI NOODLE STIR-FRY WITH CARROTS, EDAMAME, AND SCALLIONS *Shavige Baath*

Ⓥ Ⓖ Summer • Serves 2 or 3

Noodles don't usually come to mind when you think of Indian food, but shavige baath is a stir-fry traditionally made with homemade rice shavige or vermicelli, turmeric, black mustard seeds, chiles, curry leaves, coconut, and lemon. The dish is served as a light meal or breakfast. One of the most famous places in Bangalore to get shavige baath is Veena's Stores. On any afternoon, the sidewalk in front of the shop is full of locals enjoying these bright yellow noodles.

Traditionally, the noodles are broken up for easier eating and roasted before cooking so they don't stick together. You can find them prepacked like this at Indian shops. I usually use thin rice noodles or angel hair pasta and add vegetables like carrots, scallions, and edamame. When we get fresh edamame in our farm share, still on the stalk, this is the first recipe I reach for.

½ cup unsweetened grated coconut (fresh, frozen, or dried)

8 ounces thin rice noodles* or angel hair pasta

2 tablespoons plus 1 teaspoon peanut or canola oil

1 teaspoon black mustard seeds

Pinch of asafetida (hing) powder

½ teaspoon chana dal

1 teaspoon urad dal

5 or 6 fresh curry leaves

1 Indian green chile or serrano chile, finely chopped

2 scallions, both white and green parts, chopped

¼ teaspoon turmeric powder

2 carrots, peeled and julienned

1 cup shelled fresh or frozen edamame or green peas

Salt

Juice of half a lemon (about 1½ tablespoons), plus more if needed

2 tablespoons chopped cilantro leaves, plus more for garnish

SERVING OPTIONS

Chutney (pages 179 to 183)

Hot pickle (pages 185 to 189) or Brooklyn Delhi achaar

---

*In Indian shops, these noodles will be labeled as "vermicelli" and may be preroasted and broken into pieces for easier eating.

Thaw frozen coconut or place dried coconut in a little hot water to plump it up.

Break the noodles into 1-inch pieces.

Put 1 teaspoon of the oil in a wok or large frying pan over medium-low heat. Add the noodles and stir-fry them until golden brown and roasted, 3 to 4 minutes. Transfer to a plate to cool.

Cook the noodles according to the package instructions. Rice noodles usually just need to be soaked in warm water, and angel hair pasta can be cooked in boiling salted water. If making angel hair pasta, I usually rinse it in cold water afterward to keep it from overcooking.

Put the remaining 2 tablespoons of oil in a wok over medium heat. When the oil is hot and shimmering, add one black mustard seed. When the seed sizzles and pops, add the rest of the mustard seeds and the asafetida. Keep a lid handy to cover the pan while the mustard seeds are popping. When the popping starts to subside (a few seconds), immediately add the chana dal and urad dal. Stir to coat with oil and turn the heat to medium-low. Continue to stir the dals so they

evenly roast, until they turn a reddish golden brown and smell nutty, less than a minute. Rub the curry leaves between your fingers a little to release their natural oils, and drop them and the green chile into the oil. Cover immediately, as moisture from the curry leaves will cause the oil to spatter. Then stir to evenly coat everything with oil and continue to fry until the chile is less raw, 10 to 15 seconds.

Add the scallions and turmeric powder. Fry until softened, 1 to 2 minutes. Mix in the carrots and edamame with a pinch of salt. Stir-fry until the carrots are tender and the edamame is cooked through, 2 to 3 minutes. Turn the heat to low, add the coconut, and give the mixture a good stir. Immediately turn off the heat and add the cooked noodles, lemon juice, and ½ teaspoon of salt. Gently mix the noodles and vegetables. Taste for salt and lemon and adjust if needed. Mix in the chopped cilantro and garnish with more cilantro leaves.

Serve hot with chutney and hot pickle.

SPICED SPRING VEGETABLE AND COCONUT POLENTA
Uppittu or *Upma*

G Spring • Serves 3 or 4

This is my gluten-free spin on uppittu or upma, a savory South Indian semolina breakfast or light snack. In Kannada, *uppu* means "salt" and *hittu* means "flour," so *uppittu* roughly translates to "salted flour" and is sometimes referred to as upma. In place of Indian semolina flour or farina, I use polenta and pair it with crunchy spring vegetables and traditional flavors of black mustard seeds, curry leaves, chile, coconut, and lemon.

Feel free to substitute other vegetables like potato, green bell pepper, onion, grated carrot, peas, or tomatoes. Uppittu is usually served with a pat of butter or yogurt and hot pickle and sometimes a topping of fried cashews. In the past, I have used cooked quinoa or couscous in this recipe in place of polenta, so feel free to experiment with different grains as well.

½ cup unsweetened grated coconut (fresh, frozen, or dried)

1 teaspoon salt, plus more for sprinking

1 cup polenta* or medium or coarsely ground cornmeal

2 tablespoons unsalted butter

8 ounces asparagus, tough parts of spears broken off

½ cup snap peas, trimmed and stringed

1½ tablespoons coconut oil

1 teaspoon black mustard seeds

½ teaspoon chana dal

1 teaspoon urad dal

5 or 6 fresh curry leaves

½-inch piece fresh ginger, peeled and grated

1 Indian green chile or serrano chile, finely chopped

2 or 3 scallions or seasonal ramps, both white and green parts, chopped

¼ teaspoon turmeric powder

4 or 5 red radishes, trimmed and quartered

Juice of half a lemon (about 1½ tablespoons), plus more as needed

2 tablespoons chopped cilantro leaves

SERVING OPTIONS

Plain yogurt or butter

Hot pickle (pages 185 to 189) or Brooklyn Delhi achaar

---

*If using quick-cooking polenta, adjust cooking times accordingly.

Thaw frozen coconut or place dried coconut in a little hot water to plump it up.

Bring 4 cups water to a boil in a saucepan, and add the salt. Turn the heat to low and slowly whisk in the polenta until there are no lumps. Cook the polenta, partially covered, for 30 minutes, whisking it well every few minutes. When cooked, the

continued

polenta should look creamy. Add the butter and coconut and mix well. The polenta should become fluffy and lighter in color when you do this.

While the polenta is cooking, cut the asparagus into 1-inch pieces on the diagonal. Cut the snap peas into 1-inch pieces on the diagonal.

Put the oil in a wok over medium heat. When the oil is hot and shimmering, add one black mustard seed. When the seed sizzles and pops, add the rest of the mustard seeds. Keep a lid handy to cover the pan while the mustard seeds are popping. When the popping starts to subside (a few seconds), immediately add the chana dal and urad dal. Stir to coat with oil and turn the heat to medium-low.

Continue to stir the dals so they evenly roast, until they turn a reddish golden brown and smell nutty, less than a minute. Rub the curry leaves between your fingers a little to release their natural oils, and drop them, the ginger, and green chile into the oil. Cover immediately, as moisture from the curry leaves will cause the oil to spatter. Then stir to evenly coat everything with oil and continue to fry until the ginger and chile are less raw, 10 to 15 seconds.

Add the scallions and turmeric powder. Stir-fry for 1 minute on medium heat. Mix in the asparagus, snap peas, and radishes with a sprinkling of salt. Stir-fry the vegetables over high heat until tender but still crisp and just cooked through, about 3 minutes. During cooking, if the pan is looking dry, add a little water to it. Turn off the heat. Mix in the lemon juice and chopped cilantro. Taste for salt and lemon juice and adjust as needed.

Serve the polenta hot, topped with the vegetables, a dollop of plain yogurt, and a spoonful of hot pickle.

"HOTEL" SCRAMBLED EGGS

G All seasons • Serves 2

This egg scramble pays homage to the omelets my brother and I would order in hotels when we were on family vacations in India. In addition to visiting family, my parents would take us on excursions to see other parts of the country. We always looked forward to the lavish breakfast spreads in these hotels, including the Indian-style omelets cooked with green chiles, fragrant spices, and a medley of vegetables.

I made this scramble for Ben for the first time with fresh eggs from our farm share. It is divine on its own, but if you are feeling inspired, Ben and I love to eat these eggs in corn tortillas with crunchy potato hash browns, grated sharp Cheddar, a spoonful of Greek yogurt, and a Brooklyn Delhi tomato achaar.

1 tablespoon ghee (page 202) or unsalted butter

½ teaspoon black mustard seeds

2 fresh curry leaves, finely chopped

1-inch piece fresh ginger, peeled and grated

1 Indian green chile or serrano chile, minced

1 shallot, diced

¼ teaspoon turmeric powder

1 small green bell pepper, diced

1 plum tomato, diced

Salt

4 eggs

1 tablespoon whole milk (optional)

Freshly ground black pepper

2 tablespoons chopped cilantro leaves

SERVING OPTIONS

Ketchup

Brooklyn Delhi tomato achaar

In a well-seasoned cast-iron or nonstick frying pan, melt the ghee over medium heat. When melted, add one black mustard seed. When the seed sizzles and pops, add the rest of the mustard seeds. Keep a lid handy to cover the pan while the mustard seeds are popping. When the popping starts to subside (a few seconds), turn the heat down to medium-low. Rub the curry leaves between your fingers a little to release their natural oils, and drop them, the ginger, and green chile into the pan. Cover immediately, as moisture from the curry leaves will cause the ghee to spatter. Then stir to evenly coat everything with ghee, and continue to stir-fry until the ginger and chile are less raw, 10 to 15 seconds.

Add the shallot and fry until softened and translucent, a couple of minutes. Mix in the turmeric powder. Add the bell pepper and fry until it is tender but still holds its shape, 1 to 2 minutes. Toss in the tomato with a pinch of salt and cook until it is soft but still holds its shape, about 2 minutes.

Whisk the eggs in a bowl with the milk, if using, and season with salt and pepper.

Turn the heat to medium-low and stir in the eggs. Cook and stir until fluffy curds form and are cooked to your preference. Turn off the heat. Mix in the cilantro.

Serve immediately with equal parts ketchup and Brooklyn Delhi tomato achaar.

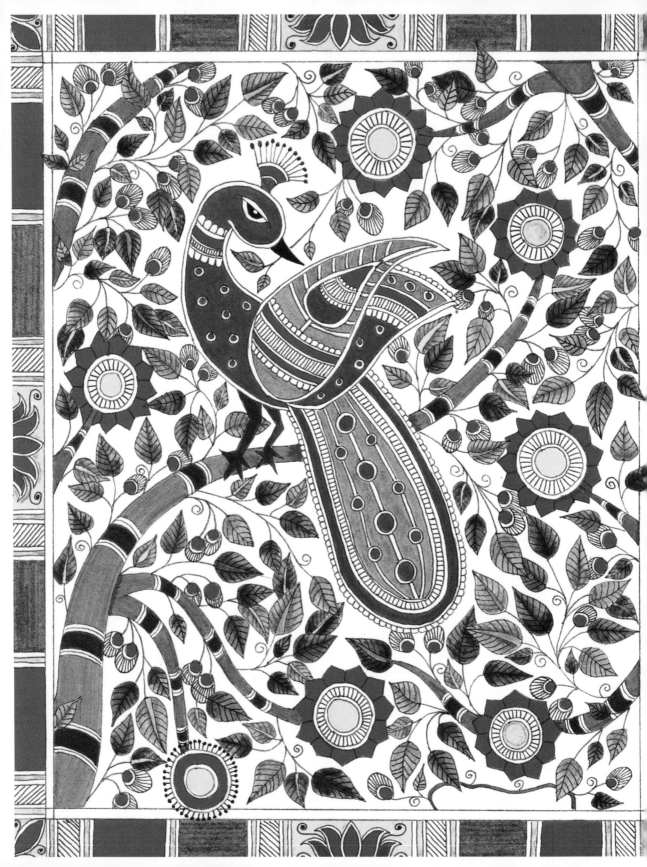

2

SALADS AND YOGURTS

You will not find lettuce, or any greens for that matter, in a South Indian salad. The salads I grew up eating were explosions of color on the plate, consisting of shredded or chopped veggies punctuated by hearty soaked lentils or sprouted beans, fresh coconut, lemon, and cilantro, and topped with fried mustard seeds, chiles, and curry leaves. I've added fruit to some of these salads—pomegranate seeds or Asian pear—to add sweetness. The salads in this chapter refresh the palate and are packed with protein and flavor.

From a young age, I thought that sweet yogurt tasted unnatural, because I had always associated yogurt with savory food. In a South Indian meal, yogurt serves as a sour component and a cooling agent. Plain yogurt is present at each meal and is sometimes accompanied by an additional yogurt dish—we love our yogurt! Yogurt raitas are prepared with a freshly cut vegetable and tempered spices, and yogurt curries are flavored with pastes made from coconut, chiles, and herbs. A tradition rooted in ayurveda is to end your meal with a small helping of rice and plain yogurt mixed together, which aids digestion and calms your stomach after a spicy meal.

SHREDDED CARROT AND LENTIL SALAD

Hesaru Bele Carrot Kosambri

  Summer, Fall • Serves 4 to 6

Kosambri is a classic Karnataka salad made with crunchy vegetables, soaked lentils, coconut, lemon, cilantro, and fried spices and chiles. It's spicy, sweet, and tangy all at once. The colorful salad is usually made on festival days or special occasions. My mother would mix all of the ingredients up with her hand, and now so do I. I'm convinced that it tastes better that way. Kosambri comes in many different forms, but this version is the one that was made most often at home. It is referred to as hesaru bele carrot kosambri, which translates from Kannada as "skinned and split mung bean and carrot salad."

I use this recipe as a template and make variations depending on what I have on hand. For instance, I sometimes use mung bean sprouts instead of the moong dal, or cut grapes instead of the coconut.

2 tablespoons moong dal or ⅓ cup mung bean sprouts (see page 65) or other green sprouts

¾ cup unsweetened grated coconut (fresh, frozen, or dried)

3 medium carrots, peeled and shredded (about 2 cups)

½ cucumber, peeled, seeded, and finely chopped

1 plum tomato, finely chopped

2 teaspoons mild-flavored oil such as canola

½ teaspoon black mustard seeds

Pinch of asafetida (hing) powder

4 or 5 fresh curry leaves

1 or 2 Indian green chiles or serrano chiles, finely chopped

Juice of half a lemon (about 1½ tablespoons), plus more as needed

¼ cup chopped cilantro leaves, plus more for garnish

½ to ¾ teaspoon salt

Wash the moong dal until the water is clear, and soak it in water for 2 to 3 hours. It should have doubled in size.

Thaw frozen coconut or place dried coconut in a little hot water to plump it up.

Drain the dal well, discarding the soaking liquid, and place in a large bowl with the carrots, cucumber, tomato, and coconut.

Put the oil in a tempering pot or a little pan over medium heat. When the oil is hot and shimmering, add one black mustard seed. When the seed sizzles and pops, add the rest of the mustard seeds and the asafetida. Keep a lid handy to cover the pan while the mustard seeds are popping. When the popping starts to subside (a few seconds), turn the heat to medium-low. Rub the curry leaves between your fingers a little to release their natural oils, and drop them and the green chile into the oil. Cover immediately, as moisture from the curry leaves will cause the oil to spatter. Then stir to evenly coat everything with oil and continue to fry until the chile is less raw, 10 to 15 seconds. Turn off the heat.

Immediately pour the oil mixture over the vegetables. To get all of the oil out of the pan, put a spoonful or two of the salad into the pan, stir, and spoon it back into the bowl.

Add the lemon juice, cilantro, and ½ teaspoon of the salt, and mix well. Taste for lemon and salt and adjust if needed. Garnish with more cilantro and serve.

RED CABBAGE AND CITRUS COLESLAW *Yalekosu Kosambri*

Ⓥ Ⓖ Fall, Winter, Spring • Serves 6

This salad is actually a variation on kosambri that my husband, Ben, first made me when we received a nice red cabbage in our farm share. We dubbed it our South Indian coleslaw. This version of the recipe has shredded red cabbage, snow peas, fennel, red onion, and peanuts in a green chile and orange vinaigrette. The secret is to shave the cabbage as finely as you can, so that the shreds absorb all of the flavors of the dressing.

Depending on the time of year, we've made alternative versions of this recipe using shredded brussels sprouts, snap peas, carrots, corn, or celery and also used different nuts, like cashews, almonds, or macadamias. Grated ginger is another good addition. Serve as a side, stuffed into shishito pepper fritters (page 148), or in tacos.

½ medium head red cabbage (about 2 pounds), trimmed, cored, and cut in half

1 small fennel bulb, trimmed

1 cup snow peas, trimmed

½ small red onion

⅓ cup raw peanuts or roasted peanuts, with or without skin

1 tablespoon peanut or canola oil

½ teaspoon black mustard seeds

Big pinch of asafetida (hing) powder

4 or 5 fresh curry leaves

1 or 2 Indian green chiles or serrano chiles, finely chopped

Juice of 2 navel oranges, or ½ cup orange juice

Grated zest of 1 orange

Juice of 1 lemon (about 3 tablespoons), plus more if needed

1 tablespoon sugar

Salt

½ cup chopped parsley or cilantro leaves, plus more for garnish

A few fennel fronds, chopped, for garnish

Finely shred the cabbage with a mandoline or sharp knife. You should have about 5 cups of cabbage. Finely shred the fennel with a mandoline or sharp knife. You should have about 1 cup of fennel. Thinly slice the snow peas on the diagonal. Thinly slice the red onion until you have about ½ cup.

Place the cabbage, fennel, snow peas, and onion in a large bowl.

If using raw peanuts, put a pan over medium heat and dry-roast the peanuts, stirring them all the while, until fragrant and golden brown, a few minutes. Set aside on a plate to cool. When cool, coarsely chop or crush the peanuts and then sprinkle with salt. If using roasted peanuts, coarsely chop or crush them.

Put the oil in a tempering pot or a little pan over medium heat. When the oil is hot and shimmering, add one black mustard seed. When the seed sizzles and pops, add the rest of the mustard seeds and the asafetida. Keep a lid handy to cover the pan while the mustard seeds are popping. When the popping starts to subside (a few seconds), turn the heat to medium-low. Rub the curry leaves between your fingers a little to release their natural oils, and drop them and the green chile into the oil. Cover immediately, as moisture from the curry leaves will cause the oil to spatter. Then stir to evenly coat everything with oil and continue to fry until the chile is less raw, 10 to 15 seconds. Turn off the heat.

Immediately pour the oil mixture over the shredded vegetables. To get all of the oil out of the pan, put a spoonful or two of the salad into the pan, stir, and then spoon it back into the bowl.

Mix in the orange juice, orange zest, lemon juice, sugar, and ½ teaspoon of salt. Stir in the chopped parsley and peanuts, saving some of each for a garnish. Taste for salt and lemon juice and adjust if needed.

You can serve the salad immediately or marinate in the fridge for an hour. Before serving, top the salad with more parsley, the reserved peanuts, and the chopped fennel fronds.

ROOT VEGETABLE AND ASIAN PEAR SALAD

 Ⓥ Ⓖ Winter • Serves 4 to 6

The idea for this salad came to me from my friend cookbook author Cathy Erway. We were preparing dinner for a pop-up at Jimmy's No. 43 in the East Village, with a menu of all Indian dishes using local produce from Evolutionary Organics. It being winter, we had a lot of root vegetable options. What I love about this recipe is that it includes vegetables that for the most part are usually roasted, so this salad gives you a different side to them.

In tossing the salad together, you can use any combination of crunchy root vegetables you have on hand, with a mix of either Asian pear or a juicy, crunchy apple like a Fuji, Honeycrisp, or Mutsu. Some good vegetable candidates are radish, daikon, carrot, celery root, kohlrabi, parsnip, rutabaga, and turnip.

¼ cup unsweetened grated coconut (fresh, frozen, or dried)

1 medium carrot, peeled

½ large turnip, peeled

1 Asian pear

2 radishes

1 tablespoon mild-flavored oil such as canola

½ teaspoon black mustard seeds

Pinch of asafetida (hing) powder

4 fresh curry leaves

1 or 2 dried red chiles, broken in half

Juice of half a lemon (about 2½ tablespoons), plus more if needed

¼ cup chopped cilantro or parsley leaves, plus more for garnish

Salt

Thaw frozen coconut or place dried coconut in a little hot water to plump it up.

Julienne the carrot, turnip, Asian pear, and radishes. Place in a large bowl. You should end up with about 5 cups.

Put the oil in a tempering pot or a little pan over medium heat. When the oil is hot and shimmering, add one black mustard seed. When the seed sizzles and pops, add the rest of the mustard seeds and the asafetida. Keep a lid handy to cover the pan while the mustard seeds are popping. When the popping starts to subside (a few seconds), turn the heat to medium-low. Rub the curry leaves between your fingers a little to release their natural oils, and drop them and the dried red chile into the oil. Cover immediately, as the moisture from the curry leaves will cause the oil to spatter. Then stir to evenly coat everything with oil, a few seconds. Turn off the heat.

Immediately pour the oil mixture over the julienned fruit and vegetables. To get all of the oil out of the pan, put a spoonful or two of the salad into the pan, stir, and then spoon it back into the bowl.

Mix in the coconut, lemon juice, cilantro, and 1 teaspoon salt. Taste for salt and lemon juice and adjust, if needed. Garnish with more cilantro and serve.

how to sprout a bean

Makes about 1 cup sprouts

Here is a method I learned from my paternal grandmother for sprouting beans, which you can apply to mung beans, chickpeas, black chickpeas, horse gram, or black-eyed peas. Sprouts are great to have around because you can use them in a variety of ways—with dosas and dals, or in salads or sandwiches. For a more expedited approach, you can purchase a sprouter.

½ cup dried beans (see headnote for suggested types)

Rinse the beans, and then immerse them in water to cover overnight. They will plump up.

The next day, rinse the beans again and drain in a colander. You can let them drain all day while you're at work.

Transfer the beans to a dish, preferably one that is flat on the bottom. Cover the dish with cheesecloth or a thin tea towel. Place in a warm spot in your kitchen. I put mine in the oven with the light on overnight.

The next morning you will have sprouts. Rinse the sprouts off and pat them dry.

Store in the refrigerator for use during the week.

CUCUMBER, SPROUTED MUNG BEAN, AND POMEGRANATE SALAD

 Spring, Summer, Fall • Serves 4

I was visiting home one winter when my mother gave me a new variation of her kosambri salad (page 61) with pomegranate seeds mixed in. Tasting it brought back a memory of driving with her in Bangalore on a street lined with huge mangrove trees and fruit carts. We stopped at one vendor and bought pomegranates, and she cut the fruit open for me at home, the seeds bright and bursting with juice.

Inspired by this memory, I came up with my own version with pomegranate, cucumber, sprouted mung beans, and coconut. This is a light, refreshing salad that has a great texture to it. If you want more heat, chop up some more fresh green chile and mix it in.

3 tablespoons unsweetened grated coconut (fresh, frozen, or dried)

1 large cucumber, peeled, seeded, and finely chopped

½ cup mung bean sprouts or other green sprouts (see page 65)

½ cup pomegranate seeds

2 teaspoons mild-flavored oil such as canola

½ teaspoon black mustard seeds

Pinch of asafetida (hing) powder

3 or 4 fresh curry leaves

1 Indian green chile or serrano chile, finely chopped

Juice of half a lime (about 1½ tablespoons), plus more if needed

2 tablespoons chopped cilantro or mint leaves, plus more for garnish

¼ to ½ teaspoon salt

Thaw frozen coconut or place dried coconut in a little hot water to plump it up.

Briefly wrap the chopped cucumber in a paper towel or dish towel to soak up the moisture.

In a large bowl, combine the drained cucumber, bean sprouts, pomegranate seeds, and coconut.

Put the oil in a tempering pot or a little pan over medium heat. When the oil is hot and shimmering, add one black mustard seed. When the seed sizzles and pops, add the rest of the mustard seeds and the asafetida. Keep a lid handy to cover the pan while the mustard seeds are popping. When the popping starts to subside (a few seconds), turn the heat to medium-low. Rub the curry leaves between your fingers a little to release their natural oils, and drop them and the green chile into the oil. Cover immediately, as moisture from the curry leaves will cause the oil to spatter. Then stir to evenly coat everything with oil and continue to fry until the chile is less raw, 10 to 15 seconds. Turn off the heat.

Immediately pour the oil mixture over the ingredients in the bowl. To get all of the oil out of the pan, put a spoonful or two of the salad into the pan, stir, and spoon it back into the bowl.

Add the lime juice, chopped cilantro, and ¼ teaspoon of the salt and mix well. Taste for salt and lime juice, and adjust if needed. Garnish with more cilantro and serve.

CHICKPEA SALAD WITH SUMMER VEGETABLES AND AVOCADO *Kadale Usali*

 Summer • Serves 4 to 6

VIBRANT INDIA

Usali is traditionally made using one type of cooked bean, such as black chickpeas, mung beans, or horse gram, and can also be prepared with the sprouted versions of these beans. Kadale kaalu usali, the black chickpea version of the salad, is usually prepared during festival days in Karnataka for prasadam, a food offering given to worshippers at Hindu temples.

This recipe is my variation on usali that I made up for a friend's potluck barbecue using regular chickpeas instead of black chickpeas. At the time, I had a can of chickpeas, an avocado, and some farm-share veggies and not a lot of time to pull something together. It's now become a staple recipe for summer picnics. I sometimes will add hearty grains like farro, wheat berries, barley, or kamut to make a complete meal.

8 ounces green (string) beans, trimmed

1 small shallot, thinly sliced into half-circles (about ¼ cup)

1 (15-ounce) can chickpeas, drained and rinsed (about 2 cups)

1 red bell pepper, cut into ½-inch pieces

1 tablespoon mild-flavored oil such as canola

½ teaspoon black mustard seeds

Pinch of asafetida (hing) powder

6 or 7 fresh curry leaves

1 or 2 Indian green chiles or serrano chiles, finely chopped

¾ to 1 teaspoon salt

2 tablespoons freshly squeezed lemon juice

½ cup chopped cilantro or parsley leaves, plus more for garnish

1 avocado, peeled and cut into cubes

Bring a saucepan of salted water to a boil. Blanch the green beans until they are bright green but still have crunch to them, about 2 minutes. Place the sliced shallot in a colander and pour the green beans and their blanching water over it. Transfer the green beans to a bowl of ice water so they don't cook further. Place the shallot in a large bowl. Drain the green beans and cut them into 1-inch pieces. Place the chickpeas, green beans, and bell pepper in the bowl with the shallot.

Put the oil in a tempering pot or a little pan over medium heat. When the oil is hot and shimmering, add one black mustard seed. When the seed sizzles and pops, add the rest of the mustard seeds and the asafetida. Keep a lid handy to cover the pan while the mustard seeds are popping. When the popping starts to subside (a few seconds), turn the heat to medium-low. Rub the curry leaves between your fingers a little to release their natural oils, and drop them and the green chile into the oil. Cover immediately, as moisture from the curry leaves will cause the oil to spatter. Then stir to evenly coat everything with oil and continue to fry until the chile is less raw, 10 to 15 seconds. Turn off the heat.

Immediately pour the oil mixture over the chickpeas and vegetables. To get all of the oil out of the pan, put a spoonful or two of the salad into the pan, stir, and spoon it back into the bowl.

Add in the salt, lemon juice, and cilantro. Gently mix in the avocado. Garnish with more cilantro and serve.

SUMMER SQUASH IN HERBY COCONUT YOGURT CURRY *Majjige Huli*

 G Summer, Fall • Serves 4

Summer is when my refrigerator is stocked to the brim with zucchini, pattypans, and yellow squash from the farm share. One year I applied my bounty to my mother's recipe for majjige huli, a green yogurt curry that she often makes with watery squashes such as ash gourd and chayote squash. This dish is traditionally made with just one type of vegetable at a time and also works well with eggplant, spinach, cucumber, potatoes, green bell pepper, okra, and green tomatoes.

In Kannada, *majjige* means "buttermilk" and *huli* means "sour." Traditionally, majjige huli is prepared with buttermilk, but it can be made with yogurt too. The dish is flavored with a paste of ground coconut, green chiles, cilantro, and spices. Roasted chana dal, which are roasted, skinned, and split black chickpeas, are also ground and used in this recipe as a thickener, but you could substitute blanched almonds for this purpose.

CURRY SAUCE

½ cup unsweetened grated coconut (fresh, frozen, or dried)

1 tablespoon roasted chana dal (chana dalia)*

½ teaspoon cumin seeds

1½ teaspoons black mustard seeds

¼ teaspoon turmeric powder

2 or 3 Indian green chiles or serrano chiles

1 cup cilantro leaves and tender stems

2 cups plain yogurt, lightly beaten by hand

SQUASH

1 pound summer squash (2 or 3 small yellow or green zucchini)

2 teaspoons mild-flavored oil such as canola

½ teaspoon black mustard seeds

Pinch of asafetida (hing) powder

1 sprig curry leaves (about 20 leaves)

1 dried red chile, broken in half

Salt

Cooked rice, for serving

Chopped cilantro leaves, for garnish

*If you have chana dal that is not roasted, soak it in hot water for 15 minutes. Otherwise, use blanched almonds or almond flour or leave it out.

To make the curry sauce: Thaw frozen coconut or place dried coconut in a little hot water to plump it up.

In a blender, grind the roasted chana dal to a powder. Add the cumin seeds, black mustard seeds, and turmeric powder and grind. Have about 1 cup of water by the blender. Next, grind the coconut and green chiles, adding a little water to help the blades along. Then add the cilantro and slowly add just enough water to keep the blender blades

continued

moving, about ½ cup, depending on the size of your blender container. Grind until you have a smooth paste, but with some texture from the grated coconut. Keep blending and scraping down the sides until you get there. When you have a nice paste, add the yogurt. Blend well so that all of the paste is incorporated.

Cut the squash in half lengthwise. Then cut each half into ½-inch-thick rounds, with large pieces cut into half again.

In a sauté pan, fit a steamer with water at a level that is just below the steamer and not touching it. Place the summer squash in the steamer basket. Cover and steam over medium heat until just tender, about 10 minutes. Immediately immerse the squash in a bowl of cold water to avoid overcooking.

Put the oil in the sauté pan over medium heat. When the oil is hot and shimmering, add one black mustard seed. When the seed sizzles and pops, add the remaining mustard seeds and the asafetida. Keep a lid handy to cover the pan while the mustard seeds are popping. When the popping starts to subside (a few seconds), turn the heat to medium-low. Rub the curry leaves between your fingers a little to release their natural oils, and drop them and the dried red chile into the oil. Cover immediately, as moisture from the curry leaves will cause the oil to spatter. Then stir to evenly coat everything with oil, a few seconds.

Mix the steamed summer squash into the pan. Next, add the curry sauce and 1 teaspoon salt. Turn the heat to medium. You want the mixture to boil once. When it does, turn the heat off.

Taste for salt and adjust as needed. Garnish with chopped cilantro leaves.

Serve with rice. The dish is served either just prepared or chilled. If eating it the next day, do not reheat before serving.

Quick Yogurt Sauce

Blend up the curry sauce ingredients to make a quick, cold yogurt sauce, perfect for spooning over most everything, including nuchinunde, steamed lentil dumplings (page 50). This sauce is referred to as hasi (raw) majjige huli. You can also add in a diced cucumber to make a flavorful yogurt raita.

BEET YOGURT RAITA

 All seasons • Serves 6 to 8

This recipe is essentially a two-for-one. It involves making a beet stir-fry, which is great on its own with a dash of lime juice, or you can continue to the next phase and combine the sauté with yogurt to make a raita. I've made it with all varieties of beets, from purple to golden. The sweetness of the beets mixes nicely with the sour yogurt, coconut, and green chiles. Shredded carrots can also be used for a variation.

Feel free to use different herbs, like chopped dill, for garnish or Greek yogurt to make the dish more diplike. This raita is a great accompaniment to rice and lentils, tacos, or even plain rice. And don't throw away those beet greens; use them in your black-eyed peas and greens stew (page 137).

3 tablespoons unsweetened grated coconut (fresh, frozen, or dried)

1 tablespoon mild-flavored oil such as canola

½ teaspoon black mustard seeds

Pinch of asafetida (hing) powder

4 fresh curry leaves

1 or 2 Indian green chiles or serrano chiles, chopped

1 medium beet, peeled and grated (about 2 cups)

¼ teaspoon turmeric powder

½ teaspoon salt

2 cups plain whole-milk yogurt, lightly beaten by hand

3 tablespoons chopped cilantro leaves, plus more for garnish

Thaw frozen coconut or place dried coconut in a little hot water to plump it up.

Put the oil in a tempering pot or a little pan over medium heat. When the oil is hot and shimmering, add one black mustard seed. When the seed sizzles and pops, add the rest of the mustard seeds and the asafetida. Keep a lid handy to cover the pan while the mustard seeds are popping. When the popping starts to subside (a few seconds), turn the heat to medium-low. Rub the curry leaves between your fingers a little to release their natural oils, and drop them and the green chile into the oil. Cover immediately, as moisture from the curry leaves will cause the oil to spatter. Then stir to evenly coat everything with oil and continue to fry until the chile is less raw, 10 to 15 seconds.

Add the shredded beet, turmeric powder, ¼ teaspoon of the salt, and a few tablespoons of water to the pan. Mix well and stir-fry over medium heat until tender and no longer raw, 8 to 10 minutes. Add a touch more water to the pan if it is looking dry. Transfer the beet to a medium bowl to cool. (To speed up the process, I sometimes put the bowl in the freezer.)

When the beet has cooled, combine it with the beaten yogurt, coconut, and chopped cilantro. Add the remaining ¼ teaspoon salt, or to taste. If my beets are super sweet, I like to balance the flavor by adding a little extra salt. Garnish with chopped cilantro and serve.

RADISH YOGURT RAITA

Ⓖ All seasons • Serves 6 to 8

Radish is one of those vegetables that you buy in a bunch and rarely use all at once, so I'm always looking for new ways to incorporate it into dishes. This recipe is one of my staples for when I have some extra ones lying around.

I never would have thought to put radish in raita if not for my mother. This is her recipe. It's a nice combination of spiciness from the radish, black mustard seeds, and chile; sweetness from the coconut; and sourness from the yogurt. Feel free to use daikon or a mix of daikon and red radishes for another variation on this recipe.

Serve as a side along with rice or chapatis (page 115) and a palya (pages 80 to 87) for example.

3 tablespoons unsweetened grated coconut (fresh, frozen, or dried)

2 or 3 small radishes, trimmed

½ small plum tomato, diced

2 cups plain yogurt, lightly beaten by hand

1 teaspoon mild-flavored oil such as canola

½ teaspoon black mustard seeds

Pinch of asafetida (hing) powder

3 fresh curry leaves

1 dried red chile, broken in half

2 tablespoons chopped cilantro leaves, plus more for garnish

Salt

Thaw frozen coconut or place dried coconut in a little hot water to plump it up.

Grate the radishes. You should have about ½ cup.

Combine the grated radishes, tomato, coconut, and yogurt in a medium bowl.

Put the oil in a tempering pot or a little pan over medium heat. When the oil is hot and shimmering, add one black mustard seed. When the seed sizzles and pops, add the rest of the mustard seeds and the asafetida. Keep a lid handy to cover the pan while the mustard seeds are popping. When the popping starts to subside (a few seconds), turn the heat to medium-low. Rub the curry leaves between your fingers a little to release their natural oils, and drop them and the dried red chile into the oil. Cover immediately, as moisture from the curry leaves will cause the oil to spatter. Then stir to evenly coat everything with oil, a few seconds. Turn off the heat.

Immediately pour the oil mixture over the raita. To get all of the oil out of the pan, put a spoonful or two of the raita into the pan, stir, and spoon it back into the bowl.

Add the cilantro and ½ teaspoon salt, and mix thoroughly. Taste and adjust the salt if needed. Garnish with chopped cilantro before serving.

KALE YOGURT RAITA

This recipe is based on a spinach raita that was prepared by my friend Asha's mom. It's also loosely inspired by Greek tzatziki, which is usually made with cucumbers, chopped garlic, and lemon. It's creamy and indulgent, and you can use it as a dip or eat it plain or with a meal.

I often make this raita with sautéed kale, using any and all varieties—curly, red, and lacinato—and have also substituted different greens such as spinach, tatsoi, or mizuna in this recipe.

You can eat the raita as a dip, or serve it as a side with rice and one of the hulis on pages 131 to 137.

1 tablespoon mild-flavored oil such as canola

¼ teaspoon black mustard seeds

¼ teaspoon cumin seeds

3 fresh curry leaves

1 Indian green chile or serrano chile, chopped

1 clove garlic, minced

2 cups stemmed, chopped kale leaves

¼ to ½ teaspoon salt

Squeeze of lemon juice

2 cups plain yogurt, lightly beaten by hand

2 tablespoons sour cream or Greek yogurt

Freshly ground black pepper

Red chile powder or paprika, for garnish

Put the oil in a small frying pan or sauté pan over medium heat. When the oil is hot and shimmering, add one black mustard seed. When the seed sizzles and pops, add the rest of the mustard seeds. Keep a lid handy to cover the pan while the mustard seeds are popping. When the popping starts to subside (a few seconds), add the cumin seeds. When the cumin seeds turn a darker shade of golden brown, turn the heat to medium-low. Rub the curry leaves between your fingers a little to release their natural oils, and drop them and the green chile into the oil. Cover immediately, as moisture from the curry leaves will cause the oil to spatter. Then stir to evenly coat everything with oil and continue to fry until the chile is less raw, 10 to 15 seconds. Stir in the garlic and sauté until fragrant, 10 to 15 seconds.

Add the kale to the pan, followed by ¼ teaspoon of the salt. Sauté until the kale is bright green in color and just wilted, 1 to 2 minutes. Add one good squeeze of lemon juice. Transfer the kale to a medium bowl and let cool. (I sometimes put it in the freezer for a few minutes if I'm in a rush.)

When the kale is cool, mix it with the yogurt, sour cream, and remaining ¼ teaspoon salt, or to taste. Garnish with a few grinds of pepper and a sprinkling of red chile powder on top before serving.

CUCUMBER, TOMATO, AND ONION YOGURT RAITA

G Spring, Summer, Fall • Serves 6 to 8

This raita transports me back to our old kitchen in New Jersey. When my mom would ask me which raita I'd like, this was it. Now when I make it, I have to stop myself from eating the whole thing in one sitting. The crunchiness of the vegetables and the coldness of the yogurt make it addictive.

I had a childhood friend who became so obsessed with this raita that she got the recipe from my mother and began making it for herself regularly. That's what this recipe does to you. This raita pairs very well with huggi, a comforting rice and lentil "risotto" (page 112) and is a perfect cooling side to any meal.

½ cucumber, peeled, seeded, and diced

½ plum tomato, diced

¼ small red onion or 1 shallot, finely chopped

2 cups plain yogurt, lightly beaten by hand

¼ teaspoon red chile powder or good cayenne pepper, plus more for garnish

½ teaspoon salt

2 tablespoons chopped cilantro leaves, plus more for garnish

1 teaspoon mild-flavored oil such as canola

½ teaspoon black mustard seeds

3 fresh curry leaves

In a medium bowl, stir together the cucumber, tomato, red onion, and yogurt. Mix in the chile powder, salt, and chopped cilantro. Taste for seasoning, and adjust the chile powder and salt as needed.

Put the oil in a tempering pot or a little pan over medium heat. When the oil is hot and shimmering, add one black mustard seed. When the seed sizzles and pops, add the rest of the mustard seeds. Keep a lid handy to cover the pan while the mustard seeds are popping. When the popping starts to subside (a few seconds), turn the heat to medium-low. Rub the curry leaves between your fingers a little to release their natural oils, and drop them into the oil. Cover immediately, as moisture from the curry leaves will cause the oil to spatter. Then stir to evenly coat the leaves with oil, a few seconds. Turn off the heat.

Immediately pour the oil mixture over the raita. To get all of the oil out of the pan, put a spoonful or two of the raita into the pan, stir, and spoon it back into the bowl.

Garnish with a sprinkle of chile powder and chopped cilantro before serving.

3

STIR-FRIES AND CURRIES

For centuries, my family has followed a vegetarian diet, with cooking traditions that celebrate the seasonal produce available. The fruit and vegetable bazaars of Bangalore feature a maze of vendors selling outstanding varieties of greens and herbs, roots for pickling, flowers, vegetables, and fruits that range from the everyday apple to the exotic rose apple. The colors and sheer abundance are mesmerizing. I'm lucky to visit India with my parents each year, and perusing these markets for what we will eat that evening is the most fun experience.

Feel free to use that same philosophy in cooking the dishes in this chapter. These recipes are meant to be flexible and applied to a variety of different produce. They really sing when you use what's fresh and seasonal.

Palya, a stir-fry that usually consists of just one fresh vegetable sautéed with chiles, dals, spices, curry leaves, coconut, and lemon, is a mainstay on the table at each meal in South India. For these preparations, a spoonful or so of dals is fried in oil to add a nutty and crunchy texture; it functions as a spice in these dishes. In addition to being used in stir-fries, vegetables are prepared in a variety of coconut-based curries in South Indian homes. I share a few of these—gojju, avial, and saagu—here as well.

POTATO STIR-FRY WITH ONION AND GINGER
Alugedde Palya

Ⓥ Ⓖ All seasons • Serves 6

This is the special potato palya or potato stir-fry that is used to fill a masala dosa (page 42). I actually serve it on its own quite a bit as well. The potatoes are spicy and tangy and cooked until they are soft enough to melt in your mouth. I've served this palya many different ways for the events I've hosted. I've put them inside a butter lettuce leaf with cilantro coconut chutney (page 179) for a spin on Asian lettuce wraps (page 145) and in vegan enchiladas.

You can also substitute steamed sweet potato, which also makes a wonderful dumpling filling. These potatoes are perfect as a side to eggs, too.

3 medium red or Yukon gold potatoes, scrubbed (about 1½ pounds)

1 teaspoon salt

2 tablespoons mild-flavored oil such as canola, plus more as needed

1 tablespoon ghee (page 202) or unsalted butter

½ teaspoon black mustard seeds

Pinch of asafetida (hing) powder

½ teaspoon chana dal

½ teaspoon urad dal

4 or 5 fresh curry leaves

2 teaspoons peeled, grated fresh ginger

1 Indian green chile or serrano chile, chopped

1 medium yellow onion, diced

¼ teaspoon turmeric powder

1 tablespoon freshly squeezed lemon juice, plus more as needed

2 tablespoons chopped cilantro leaves

Place the potatoes in a pot and add water to cover by 2 inches. Add the salt to the water and boil over medium-high heat until the potatoes are cooked through and tender, about 15 minutes. Drain the potatoes and let them cool. When cool, coarsely chop the potatoes into bite-size pieces.

Put the oil and ghee in a wok or large frying pan over medium heat. When the oil is hot and shimmering, add one black mustard seed. When the seed sizzles and pops, add the rest of the mustard seeds and asafetida. Keep a lid handy to cover the pan while the mustard seeds are popping. When the popping starts to subside (a few seconds), immediately add the chana dal and urad dal. Stir to coat with oil, and turn the heat to medium-low. Continue to stir the dals so they evenly roast, until they turn a reddish golden brown and smell nutty, less than a minute. Rub the curry leaves between your fingers a little to release their natural oils, and drop them, the ginger, and green chile into the oil. Cover immediately, as moisture from the curry leaves will cause the oil to spatter. Then stir to evenly coat everything with oil and continue to fry until the ginger and chile are less raw, 10 to 15 seconds.

Add the onion and turmeric powder to the pan. Turn the heat to medium. Mix well and cook until the onion is softened and translucent. Mix in the potato and stir-fry until they start to become soft and mashable. If the pan is getting dry, add a little oil. Turn off the heat. Mix in the lemon juice and cilantro. Taste for lemon juice and salt and adjust if needed before serving.

CABBAGE STIR-FRY WITH LEMON AND CURRY LEAVES
Yalekosu Palya

 All seasons • Serves 4 to 6

I've made this stir-fry with a variety of cabbages that we get in our farm share, including savoy and napa, but it's also quite delicious with regular old green or purple cabbage. This version of palya is flavored with fried black mustard seeds, dals, curry leaves, and red chiles and finished with coconut and lemon.

Feel free to substitute fresh green chiles for the dried ones, or to add fresh peas to introduce some sweetness into the mix. I've also used boiled and cubed beets and chopped bok choy and shredded Brussels sprouts in this recipe in place of cabbage for a variation. Serve this palya as a side with rice, saaru (pages 125 and 128), and yogurt, or with chapatis (page 115).

¼ cup unsweetened grated coconut (fresh, frozen, or dried)

1 small cabbage, trimmed and cored (about 1½ pounds)

2 tablespoons mild-flavored oil such as canola

½ teaspoon black mustard seeds

Pinch of asafetida (hing) powder

½ teaspoon chana dal

½ teaspoon urad dal

½ sprig curry leaves (about 10 leaves)

1 or 2 dried red chiles, broken in half

¼ teaspoon turmeric powder

¾ to 1 teaspoon salt

Juice of half a lemon (about 1½ tablespoons), plus more as needed

2 tablespoons chopped cilantro leaves

Thaw frozen coconut or place dried coconut in a little hot water to plump it up.

Finely chop the cabbage. You will end up with about 8 cups.

Put the oil a wok or large frying pan over medium heat. When the oil is hot and shimmering, add one black mustard seed. When the seed sizzles and pops, add the rest of the mustard seeds and the asafetida. Keep a lid handy to cover the pan while the mustard seeds are popping. When the popping starts to subside (a few seconds), immediately add the chana dal and urad dal. Stir to coat with oil, and turn the heat to medium-low. Continue to stir the dals so they evenly roast, until they turn a reddish golden brown and smell nutty, less than a minute. Rub the curry leaves between your fingers a little to release their natural oils, and drop them and the dried red chiles into the oil. Cover immediately, as moisture from the curry leaves will cause the oil to spatter. Then stir to evenly coat everything with oil, a few seconds.

Add the turmeric powder to the pan, immediately followed by the chopped cabbage and ¾ teaspoon of the salt. Stir-fry until the cabbage is tender and cooked through, about 3 minutes. The cabbage should be wilty and soft, with just a little crunch to it. Add the coconut and stir-fry for another minute. Turn off the heat. Mix in the lemon juice and chopped cilantro. Taste for lemon juice and salt and adjust if needed before serving.

GREEN BEAN AND COCONUT STIR-FRY *Huralikayi Palya*

 V G Summer • Serves 4

Green beans palya is a classic South Indian stir-fry. It's known throughout the region by different names, with slight variations in preparation. This is just one of the ways I like to make it. The beans are cut into quarter-inch pieces and seasoned with coconut, lemon, and a mixture of fried mustard seeds, curry leaves, and chiles.

In our family, we also add a spoonful of huli or sambar powder for more flavor. I grew up eating this stir-fry mixed with rice and saaru (page 127), but it also makes a great side. I've made this recipe with chopped asparagus and fiddlehead ferns, which work perfectly.

Thaw frozen coconut or place dried coconut in a little hot water to plump it up.

Put the oil in a wok or large frying pan over medium heat. When the oil is hot and shimmering, add one black mustard seed. When the seed sizzles and pops, add the rest of the mustard seeds and the asafetida. Keep a lid handy to cover the pan while the mustard seeds are popping. When the popping starts to subside (a few seconds), turn the heat to medium-low. Rub the curry leaves between your fingers a little to release their natural oils, and drop them and the dried red chile into the oil. Cover immediately, as moisture from the curry leaves will cause the oil to spatter. Then stir to evenly coat everything with oil, a few seconds.

Add the green beans and turmeric powder to the pan and mix well. Mix in the salt and stir-fry for a minute on medium heat. Then add a couple table-spoons of water. Turn the heat to medium-low, cover, and cook the beans until tender and cooked through, 4 to 5 minutes. Mix in the huli powder and cook for 2 minutes more. Stir in the coconut and cook everything for another minute. Turn off the heat. Mix in the lemon juice. Taste for lemon juice and salt and adjust if needed. Garnish with chopped cilantro before serving.

¼ cup unsweetened grated coconut (fresh, frozen, or dried)

1 tablespoon mild-flavored oil such as canola

½ teaspoon black mustard seeds

Pinch of asafetida (hing) powder

4 or 5 fresh curry leaves

1 dried red chile, broken in half

1 pound green (string) beans, trimmed and cut into ¼-inch pieces

¼ teaspoon turmeric powder

¾ teaspoon salt

1 teaspoon huli powder (page 196) or store-bought sambar powder

1 tablespoon freshly squeezed lemon juice, plus more as needed

Chopped cilantro leaves, for garnish

"VANGI BAATH" ROASTED BRUSSELS SPROUTS AND CAULIFLOWER

(G) Fall, Winter • Serves 4 to 6

Vangi baath (page 106) is actually a South Indian eggplant rice, but the spice blend used to make that dish is a fantastic way to flavor roasted vegetables. The spice powder is made from roasted and ground dals, coriander, cloves, cinnamon, and chiles. I've provided a recipe, or you can buy the blend ready-made at an Indian shop or online.

I first discovered how delicious vangi baath powder is on roasted vegetables when I was coming up with a menu for one of my pop-up dinners. For that event, I roasted butternut squash and cauliflower with vangi baath powder, and since then I've used it to roast tons of different types of vegetables. In the fall we get brussels sprouts still on the stalk from our farm share, and I pair them with cauliflower to make this recipe. I like to serve this as a side over brown rice or farro with a dollop of plain yogurt and Brooklyn Delhi achaar or hot pickle (pages 185 to 189).

Preheat the oven to 400°F.

In a large bowl, combine the oil and salt. Add the brussels sprouts and cauliflower to the bowl and toss to coat with the oil mixture. Place in a single layer on a rimmed baking sheet, with the brussels sprouts cut-side down, and place in the oven.

Roast the vegetables for 25 minutes undisturbed. While vegetables are roasting, stir the ghee and vangi baath powder together in a small bowl.

After 25 minutes of roasting, take the vegetables out of the oven. Drizzle the ghee mixture over vegetables on the pan and stir to coat. Place the vegetables back in the oven and roast for another 5 minutes. When done, the vegetables should be tender on the inside and browned on the outside and there should be some crisped leaves from the sprouts scattered about on the tray. Oven temperatures vary, so yours may take a little less or more time to get to this point.

Take the roasted vegetables out of the oven to cool. Sprinkle additional salt on top of the vegetables before serving.

3 tablespoons mild-flavored oil such as canola

1 teaspoon salt, plus more for sprinkling

1 pound brussels sprouts, trimmed and halved

1 medium cauliflower (about 1 pound of florets), trimmed and cut into bite-size pieces

1 tablespoon melted ghee (page 202) or butter

1 tablespoon vangi baath powder, homemade (page 198) or store-bought*

*You can substitute huli powder (page 196) or store-bought sambar powder.

STIR-FRIED CORN WITH BASIL AND LEEKS *Jolada Palya*

Ⓥ Ⓖ Summer, Fall • Serves 4

Nothing is more exciting than ripping open the first corn of summer. Growing up, we'd eat corn two ways: either roasted straight on the gas stove or shaved off the cob and stir-fried. Fresh corn really doesn't need much. In the thick of summer, I shave it off the cob and eat it raw in salads.

My mother would sauté the fresh kernels in a little butter with cumin seed, black pepper, lemon, and cilantro. I've adapted her recipe by using chopped basil and leeks I received in my farm share one year; simple to prepare but bursting with summer flavors. This dish is great as a hot side and also delicious cold and mixed into salads.

Put the ghee in a wok or large frying pan over medium heat. When it is melted, add one cumin seed. When the seed moves slightly or sizzles, add the rest of the cumin seeds. When the cumin seeds start to brown (a few seconds), add the leek. Stir-fry for about 2 minutes, until the leek is fragrant and soft. Stir in the corn kernels, black pepper, and ¼ teaspoon of the salt.

Turn the heat to medium-low and sauté until the corn is cooked to your preference, 2 to 3 minutes. I find the fresher the corn, the less you need to cook it. Turn off the heat. Mix in the lemon juice and basil. Taste for lemon juice and salt and adjust if needed before serving.

1 tablespoon ghee (page 202) or unsalted butter

½ teaspoon cumin seeds

1 small leek, finely chopped

Kernels cut from 4 ears corn (3 to 4 cups)

½ teaspoon freshly ground black pepper

¼ to ½ teaspoon salt

1 tablespoon freshly squeezed lemon juice, plus more as needed

2 tablespoons chopped basil leaves

SCALLIONS IN SPICY, SOUR, AND SWEET SAUCE *Eerulli Kavu Gojju*

 Summer, Fall • Serves 4

Gojju is a cross between a curry and a condiment. It consists of one or two vegetables flavored with a curry paste of roasted lentils, spices, chiles, coconut and tamarind, and a little jaggery or unrefined cane sugar. My version is just like my mother's, and I love it on a piece of buttered toast, with chapatis, or rolled in a corn tortilla with a dollop of plain yogurt on top. You can also mix it into hot rice topped with yogurt raita or plain yogurt.

In India, young spring onions that still have their white flowers attached are used in this recipe. Fresh scallions, or green onions, are a good substitute, and I also use ramps or garlic scapes when we get them in our farm share. Green bell pepper also pairs well with this preparation.

CURRY PASTE

¾ cup unsweetened grated coconut (fresh, frozen, or dried)

1 tablespoon roasted chana dal (chana dalia)*

¼ teaspoon black mustard seeds

Pinch of asafetida (hing) powder

2 or 3 Indian green chiles or serrano chiles

¼ cup cilantro sprigs, leaves and thin stems

½ to 1 teaspoon tamarind paste, plus more as needed

½ to ¾ cup water

2 bunches or 12 to 14 scallions

1½ tablespoons mild-flavored oil such as canola

½ teaspoon black mustard seeds

Pinch of asafetida (hing) powder

¼ teaspoon roasted fenugreek seed powder (page 199; optional)

3 or 4 fresh curry leaves

1 dried red chile

¼ teaspoon turmeric powder

½ to ¾ teaspoon salt

1 to 2 teaspoons jaggery or brown sugar, plus more as needed

SERVING OPTIONS

Buttered toast, chapatis (page 115), or tortillas

Cooked rice with plain yogurt or raita (pages 72 to 76)

---

*If you have chana dal that is not roasted, you can soak it in hot water for 15 minutes. Otherwise, use blanched almonds or almond flour or leave it out.

To make the curry paste: Thaw frozen coconut or place dried coconut in a little hot water to plump it up.

A small blender, like a Magic Bullet, is best for making this paste. If you have a regular-size blender, you may need to use more water to pulverize the ingredients. Place the roasted chana dal, black mustard seeds, and asafetida in the blender and grind them to a powder. Next add the green chiles, cilantro, tamarind paste, coconut, and enough of the water to get the blender blades going to make a smooth paste that still has texture from the grated coconut. Keep blending and scraping down the sides until you get there.

Chop the white and green parts of the scallions. You will end up with about 3 cups.

Put the oil in a sauté pan over medium heat. When the oil is hot and shimmering, add one black mustard seed. When the seed sizzles and pops, add the rest of the mustard seeds and the asafetida. Keep a lid handy to cover the pan while the mustard seeds are popping. When the popping starts to subside (a few seconds), turn the heat to medium-low. Rub the curry leaves between your fingers a little to release their natural oils, and drop them and the dried red chile into the oil. Cover immediately, as moisture from the curry leaves will cause the oil to spatter. Then stir to evenly coat everything with oil, a few seconds.

Add the scallions, turmeric powder, and roasted fenugreek seed powder, if using, to the pan and sauté over medium heat for a couple of minutes. Add the curry paste, ½ teaspoon of the salt, and 1 teaspoon of the jaggery. Bring the mixture to a boil and then simmer for about 2 minutes, adding additional water if needed.

Taste the gojju; it should be a mix of tangy, spicy, and sweet. Add tamarind paste, jaggery, or salt to adjust as needed, and simmer another minute or two to meld the flavors. The gojju will thicken as it cools. (I like this gojju to have a consistency similar to a chunky guacamole, so I can pile it on a piece of toast or roll it into a chapati or tortilla easily.)

Serve hot with toast, chapatis, or tortillas, or on rice with plain yogurt or raita on the side.

PINEAPPLE AND PEPPERS IN RED COCONUT CURRY

Ananas Gojju

Ⓥ Ⓖ Summer, Fall • Serves 4

This version of gojju is made with red chiles and curry leaves in a tamarind-coconut sauce. My mother would prepare this dish with eggplant and green bell peppers, okra, bitter gourd, tomatoes, or sweet pumpkin. My take on it uses pineapple and red bell peppers. I've also made this gojju with roasted and cubed butternut squash; there's another version I make on page 88.

CURRY PASTE

¾ cup unsweetened grated coconut (fresh, frozen, or dried)

1 tablespoon roasted chana dal (chana dalia)*

¼ teaspoon black mustard seeds

Pinch of asafetida (hing) powder

2 or 3 dried red chiles

3 or 4 fresh curry leaves

½ to ¾ cup water

1 tablespoon mild-flavored oil such as canola

½ teaspoon black mustard seeds

Pinch of asafetida (hing) powder

3 or 4 fresh curry leaves

1 dried red chile, broken in half

½ small pineapple, cut into ½-inch cubes (about 2 cups)

1 small red bell pepper, cut into ½-inch squares

¼ teaspoon turmeric powder

¼ teaspoon roasted fenugreek seed powder (page 199; optional)

1 cup water, plus more as needed

1 teaspoon tamarind paste, plus more as needed

1 to 2 teaspoons jaggery or brown sugar, plus more as needed

¾ to 1 teaspoon salt

Chopped cilantro leaves, for garnish

Chapatis (page 115), tortillas, or cooked rice, for serving

*If you have chana dal that is not roasted, you can soak it in hot water for 15 minutes. Otherwise, use blanched almonds or almond flour or leave it out.

To make the curry paste: Thaw frozen coconut or place dried coconut in a little hot water to plump it up.

A small blender, like a Magic Bullet, is best for making this paste. If you have a regular-size blender, you may need to use more water to pulverize the ingredients. Place the roasted chana dal, black mustard seeds, and asafetida in the blender and grind them to a powder. Next add the red chiles and grind them. Add the curry leaves, coconut, and enough of the water to get the blender blades going to make a paste. Keep blending and scraping down the sides until you get there.

Put the oil in a sauté pan over medium heat. When the oil is hot and shimmering, add one black mustard seed. When the seed sizzles and pops, add the rest of the mustard seeds and the asafetida. Keep a lid handy to cover the pan while the mustard seeds are popping. When the popping starts to subside (a few seconds), turn the heat to medium-low. Rub the curry leaves between your fingers a little to release their natural oils, drop them and the dried red chile into the oil. Cover immediately, as moisture from the curry leaves will cause the oil to spatter. Then stir to evenly coat everything with oil, a few seconds.

Add the pineapple, bell pepper, turmeric powder, and roasted fenugreek seed powder, if using, and sauté until the pineapple and bell pepper are just tender, 2 to 3 minutes.

continued

PINEAPPLE AND PEPPERS IN RED COCONUT CURRY *continued*

Add ½ cup of the water and the tamarind, 1 teaspoon of the jaggery, and ¾ teaspoon of the salt to the pan. Bring to a boil and simmer for 2 to 3 minutes. Add the curry paste with the remaining ½ cup water. Bring to a boil and let the mixture simmer over medium heat for about 5 minutes.

Taste the gojju; it should be a mix of tangy, spicy, and sweet. Add tamarind paste, jaggery, or salt to adjust as needed, and simmer for another minute or two to meld the flavors.

During this time, add more water to get to your desired consistency. (If you are planning on serving the gojju with rice, a gravy consistency is better; with bread or roti, a thicker consistency, like a loose coconut chutney, is preferred.) Turn off the heat. The gojju will thicken up a bit.

Garnish with chopped cilantro. Serve hot with chapatis, tortillas, or rice.

KERALA COCONUT VEGETABLE CURRY *Avial*

V G Summer, Fall • Serves 4

Avial has its origins in the South Indian state of Kerala, but you will find variations of it in Karnataka homes as well. This recipe is one I adapted from my mother's childhood friend, Lakshmi Viswanathan. She learned it from her husband and mother-in-law, who are from Kerala.

When Ben and I were in Kerala for our honeymoon, we tasted many different versions of avial, from thick to soupy, all made with different combinations of vegetables. Lakshmi usually makes hers with a tender vegetable like drumstick (a fibrous South Indian green vegetable); a starchy, chewy vegetable like plantain; a crunchy vegetable like carrot; and a sour vegetable like raw green mango. She noted that the seasoning of coconut oil at the end gives the dish a distinct Kerala flavor. I've incorporated some of the traditional vegetables with others that complement the mix of flavors.

CURRY PASTE

½ cup unsweetened grated coconut (fresh, frozen, or dried)

1 tablespoon cumin seeds

3 or 4 Indian green chiles or serrano chiles

About ½ cup water

1 cup sliced carrots, cut into ¼- to 1-inch-thick disks

¾ teaspoon salt

1 sprig curry leaves (about 20 leaves) or cilantro leaves

1 cup sliced summer squash such as zucchini, cut into ¼-inch-thick pieces

1 cup cauliflower florets, cut into bite-size pieces

1 cup green (string) beans, cut into 1-inch pieces

1 cup plain yogurt, beaten by hand

1 tablespoon coconut oil, just melted

Cooked rice or other grain, for serving

To make the curry paste: Thaw frozen coconut or place dried coconut in hot water to plump it up.

A small blender, like a Magic Bullet, is best for making this paste. If you have a regular-size blender, you may need to use more water to pulverize the ingredients. Place the cumin seeds in the blender and grind them to a powder. Next add the green chiles and blend. Add the coconut and enough of the water to make a smooth paste. Keep blending and scraping down the sides until you get there.

Add the carrots to a soup pot with enough water to just cover them. Mix in the salt and curry leaves. Bring to a boil, then simmer the carrots over medium heat until tender but not fully cooked through, a few minutes. Add the summer squash and cauliflower and enough water to just cover. Simmer for a few minutes over medium heat, until just tender. Add the green beans and simmer for another minute. Since the vegetables will simmer for a few minutes more in the next phase of the recipe, it's all right if they are not fully cooked at this point. Turn off the heat.

Pour the curry paste on top of the vegetables and their cooking water, and mix well. (Adjust the thickness of the gravy with water, but keep in mind you will be mixing in yogurt, which will loosen up the curry.) Simmer until the flavors meld and the vegetables are cooked through, a few minutes. Turn off the heat and let cool to room temperature. Add the yogurt and mix well. Pour the coconut oil over the curry, taste for salt and adjust if needed. Serve over rice or another grain.

KARNATAKA COCONUT VEGETABLE CURRY *Saagu*

 V G All seasons • Serves 4

Saagu is a recipe originating in my family's state of Karnataka and is a popular item on South Indian restaurant menus. It is a vegetable-coconut curry flavored with cilantro and aromatic spices like cinnamon, cloves, and coriander. It is most often paired with poori, a deep-fried puffy bread from North India. When I'm making saagu at home, I eat it with chapati, a North Indian flatbread that does not require deep-frying. This recipe is adapted from my Auntie Usha.

Traditionally, saagu is prepared with a medley of vegetables, such as potatoes, green beans, peas, carrots, cauliflower, kohlrabi, chayote squash, and spinach. For this recipe, you can use about 2 cups of any combination of vegetables that you like. This is the perfect recipe to make a day ahead so the flavors set in.

CURRY PASTE

¾ cup unsweetened grated coconut (fresh, frozen, or dried)

1 tablespoon roasted chana dal (chana dalia)*

1½ teaspoons coriander seeds

¼ teaspoon cumin seeds

½-inch piece cinnamon stick, or ¼ teaspoon ground cinnamon

2 cloves

1 teaspoon peeled, grated fresh ginger

2 to 4 Indian green chiles or serrano chiles

½ cup cilantro leaves

About ½ cup water

½ cup sliced carrots, cut into ¼-inch-thick disks

¾ to 1 teaspoon salt

1 cup broccoli florets, in bite-size pieces

2 tablespoons mild-flavored oil such as canola

½ teaspoon black mustard seeds

Pinch of asafetida (hing) powder

4 or 5 fresh curry leaves

1 dried red chile, broken in half

½ medium yellow onion, diced

¼ teaspoon turmeric powder

½ cup fresh or frozen green peas, shelled or thawed

Chopped cilantro leaves, for garnish

Chapatis (page 115), rava idli (page 48), or cooked rice, for serving

---

*If you have chana dal that is not roasted, you can soak it in hot water for 15 minutes. Otherwise, use blanched almonds or almond flour, or leave it out.

To make the curry paste: Thaw frozen coconut or place dried coconut in a little hot water to plump it up.

A small blender, like a Magic Bullet, is best for making this paste. If you have a regular-size blender, you may need to use more water to pulverize the

continued

STIR-FRIES AND CURRIES

ingredients. Place the roasted chana dal, coriander seeds, cumin seeds, cinnamon, and cloves in the blender, and grind them to a powder. Next add the ginger and green chiles and grind them. Add the coconut and cilantro and just enough of the water to get the blades going and make a paste. Keep blending and scraping down the sides until you get there.

Add the sliced carrots to a medium saucepan with enough water to just cover them. Add ½ teaspoon of the salt to the water. Bring to a boil, then simmer the carrots over medium heat until just tender, a few minutes. Add the broccoli with enough water to cover and simmer until just tender, a couple of minutes. Since the vegetables will simmer for a few minutes more in the next phase of the recipe, it's fine if they are not fully cooked at this point. Turn off the heat. Strain the vegetables so they do not overcook, reserving their cooking water. Alternatively, you can steam the vegetables until just tender, if you prefer.

Put the oil in a heavy-bottomed pot over medium heat. When the oil is hot and shimmering, add one black mustard seed. When the seed sizzles and pops, add the rest of the mustard seeds and the asafetida. Keep a lid handy to cover the pan while the mustard seeds are popping. When the popping starts to subside (a few seconds), turn the heat to medium-low. Rub the curry leaves between your fingers a little to release their natural oils, and drop them and the dried red chile into the oil. Cover immediately, as moisture from the curry leaves will cause the oil to spatter. Then stir to evenly coat everything with oil, a few seconds.

Add the diced onion to the pot and fry over medium heat until softened and translucent, a couple of minutes. Mix in the turmeric powder. Add the curry paste to the pot and mix well. Continue to cook for a couple of minutes. Add the simmered vegetables, peas, and enough reserved vegetable water to get your desired consistency. Season with the remaining ¼ to ½ teaspoon salt. This dish is thicker than a soup, more like a loose gravy. Simmer until the vegetables are cooked through but still hold their shape, a few minutes more. Garnish with chopped cilantro. Serve with chapatis, rava idli, or rice.

4

RICE AND BREAD

Rice, or anna in Kannada, is a farm staple that thrives in the lush southern regions of India that are prone to seasonal monsoons. A South Indian meal is not a meal without rice. Countless varieties are grown, from a small-grained rice referred to as sanna akki that is starch-heavy and sticks easily to brothy soups like saaru (pages 125 and 127) to the longer-grained types that are used in making dishes like vangi baath, an eggplant rice (page 106). Rice is sacred in this region. In Hindu temples in the South, chitranna (page 103)—sour rice flavored with tamarind, lemon, or green mango—is served as prasadam, an offering of food to temple visitors.

Although rice is eaten every day, breads are also prepared in South Indian homes, albeit on a less frequent basis. Many of the flatbreads such as chapati (page 115) are largely borrowed from the cuisine of North India, where wheat grows in abundance. You will also find a variety of yeasted breads and buns (page 116), in addition to "biscuits" or savory shortbreads (page 119), in bakeries throughout Bangalore.

MY PARENTS' STEAMED BASMATI RICE

Ⓥ Ⓖ All seasons • Serves 3 or 4; makes about 4 cups

I grew up eating basmati rice, which is a North Indian variety. While not traditionally used in South Indian dishes, I prefer its flavor and long grains. I recommend purchasing Dehraduni basmati rice, which is available at most Indian shops and online.

My parents steam their rice, and I have to admit it has spoiled me forever. Essentially they use a double-boiler method, which prevents any burning or rice sticking to the bottom of the pan. The result is the most divine rice you will ever have—perfectly cooked, with separate grains and fluffy. I thought I would share their recipe because it will drastically change your rice game.

I often make a double batch and, with the leftovers, make a flavored rice recipe (pages 103 to 112) another day. I generally do not add salt when cooking my rice because I usually pair it with food that is quite well seasoned, or I season it later if making a stir-fry from it. If I am making rice for a special occasion, I will sometimes mix 1 tablespoon of oil or melted butter with the drained rice before cooking it.

When I want to add a bit of brightness on the table, I mix a little turmeric powder with the rice and water before cooking. This little addition makes your rice more fluffy, healthful, and colorful.

1 cup basmati rice, preferably Dehraduni*

⅛ teaspoon turmeric powder (optional)

---

*Since the Dehraduni variety of basmati rice has a very long grain, it yields about four times its dry quantity, but most other varieties of basmati or long-grained jasmine rice yield about three times their dry quantity.

Wash the rice in several changes of water until the water runs clear. Soak the rice in water, generously covered, for at least 30 minutes. Drain thoroughly, using a fine-mesh sieve.

Place the rice and 1½ cups water in a flat, shallow stainless steel container. (I use the circular one that came with my pressure cooker from the Indian shop.) A stainless steel cake or pie pan would work and I have also made this recipe in a stainless steel mixing bowl. Mix in the turmeric powder, if using.

Place a flat steamer plate or a steam basket on the bottom of a stockpot. Add water to the stockpot so that it covers the plate or basket by at least ½ inch. Place the container with the rice on top of the steamer plate. Turn the heat to high. When you see small bubbles forming rapidly around the rice container, cover the pot and turn the heat to medium.

Steam until the rice is cooked through and there is no water left in the rice container, about 20 minutes. Turn off the heat. Remove the stockpot from the stove and leave it covered for 10 minutes, to allow the grains to separate. Fluff with a fork before serving.

SIMPLE BASMATI RICE

  All seasons • Serves 3 or 4; makes about 4 cups

This recipe for cooking rice is an alternative to the double boiler method used in the previous recipe.

1 cup basmati rice, preferably Dehraduni*

⅛ teaspoon turmeric powder (optional)

---

*Since the Dehraduni variety of basmati rice has a very long grain, it yields about four times its dry quantity, but most other varieties of basmati or long-grained jasmine rice yield about three times their dry quantity.

Wash the rice in several changes of water until the water runs clear. Soak the rice in water, generously covered, for at least 30 minutes. Drain thoroughly, using a fine-mesh sieve.

Place the rice and 1¾ cups water in a medium saucepan. Mix in the turmeric powder, if using. Place the saucepan over high heat and bring to a boil. Once the water is boiling, cover the saucepan and turn the heat to the lowest setting on your stove.

Cook until the rice is tender and there is no water left in the pan, about 15 minutes. Turn off the heat. Remove the saucepan from the stove and leave it covered for 10 minutes, to allow the grains to separate. Fluff with a fork before serving.

LEMON PEANUT RICE *Nimbehannu Chitranna*

  All seasons • Serves 4

Nimbehannu chitranna, or lemon peanut rice, is a specialty of South Karnataka made with coconut, peanuts, and cilantro. It is prepared on auspicious occasions and served at temples, but it's also the perfect festive and colorful dish for a picnic or potluck. There are numerous variations of chitranna, a rice dish that is usually sour and flavored with either lemon, lime, green mango, or tamarind. I sometimes add sautéed shredded red cabbage and carrot right before adding the rice.

4 cups cooked turmeric rice (page 100 or 101); substitute jasmine rice for the basmati if you prefer*

¼ cup unsweetened grated coconut (fresh, frozen, or dried)**

2 tablespoons plus 1 teaspoon mild-flavored oil such as canola

¼ cup raw peanuts or unsalted roasted peanuts, preferably with skin

½ teaspoon black mustard seeds

Pinch of asafetida (hing) powder

1 teaspoon chana dal

1 teaspoon urad dal

4 or 5 fresh curry leaves

1 dried red chile, broken in half

½ to ¾ teaspoon salt

Juice of 1 lemon (about 3 tablespoons), plus more as needed

2 tablespoons chopped cilantro leaves, plus more for garnish

SERVING OPTIONS

Raita (pages 72 to 76; optional) or plain yogurt

Hot pickle (pages 185 to 189) or Brooklyn Delhi achaar

*Leftover rice or rice cooled completely on a sheet pan works best in this recipe.

** Thaw frozen coconut or place dried coconut in a little hot water to plump it.

Put 1 teaspoon of the oil in a wok or large frying pan over medium heat. Add the peanuts to the wok, stirring until they are fragrant and turn golden brown, a few minutes. Set aside on a plate lined with a paper towel.

Coat the bottom of the wok with the remaining 2 tablespoons oil and place over medium heat. When the oil is hot and shimmering, add one black mustard seed. When the seed sizzles and pops, add the rest of the mustard seeds and the asafetida. Keep a lid handy to cover the pan while the mustard seeds are popping. When the popping starts to subside (a few seconds), immediately add the chana dal and urad dal. Stir to coat with oil, and turn the heat to medium-low. Continue to stir the dals so they evenly roast, until they turn a reddish golden brown and smell nutty, less than a minute. Rub the curry leaves between your fingers a little to release their natural oils, and drop them and the dried red chile into the oil. Cover immediately, as moisture from the curry leaves will cause the oil to spatter. Then stir to evenly coat everything with oil, a few seconds.

Add the cooked rice and ½ teaspoon of the salt to the wok and mix well. Stir-fry for 1 to 2 minutes. Stir in the coconut and fry for another minute. Turn off the heat. Stir in the lemon juice and chopped cilantro. Stir in the peanuts. Taste for salt and lemon juice and adjust as needed. Garnish with more cilantro. Serve hot with raita and hot pickle.

LIME DILL RICE WITH PISTACHIOS

Nimbehannu Sabseege Soppina Baath

Ⓥ Ⓖ Summer, Fall • Serves 4

I often get a bunch of dill in our farm share. Recipes usually call for only a tablespoon or two, which leaves me with most of the bunch unused. Lime dill rice is the perfect way to use it all up in one go, as dill is the star. Here you cook the leaves down, giving them a milder flavor.

You can make this with lemon instead of lime, and peanuts or cashews lightly fried in oil instead of pistachios. Vangi baath powder or huli powder add a spicy dimension, or I sometimes add ¼ cup of grated coconut or green peas to add sweetness.

4 cups cooked turmeric rice (page 100 or 101); substitute jasmine rice for the basmati if you prefer*

2 tablespoons mild-flavored oil such as canola

½ teaspoon black mustard seeds

Pinch of asafetida (hing) powder

1 teaspoon chana dal

1 teaspoon urad dal

5 fresh curry leaves

1 dried red chile, broken in half

1 large shallot or ½ medium yellow onion, finely chopped

Small bunch of dill, tough stalks removed, chopped

½ to ¾ teaspoon salt

1 teaspoon vangi baath powder (page 198), huli powder (page 196), or store-bought sambar powder (optional)

¼ cup shelled pistachios, lightly toasted and coarsely chopped

Juice of half a lime (about 1½ tablespoons), plus more as needed

SERVING OPTIONS

Raita (pages 72 to 76; optional) or plain yogurt

Hot pickle (pages 185 to 189) or Brooklyn Delhi achaar

*Leftover rice or rice cooled completely on a sheet pan works best in this recipe.

Coat the bottom of a wok with the oil and place over medium heat. When the oil is hot and shimmering, add one black mustard seed. When the seed sizzles and pops, add the rest of the mustard seeds and the asafetida. Keep a lid handy to cover the pan while the mustard seeds are popping. When the popping starts to subside (a few seconds), immediately add the chana dal and urad dal. Stir to coat with oil, and turn the heat to medium-low. Continue to stir the dals so they evenly roast, until they turn a reddish golden brown and smell nutty, less than a minute. Rub the curry leaves between your fingers a little to release their natural oils, and drop them and the dried red chile into the oil. Cover immediately, as moisture from the curry leaves will cause the oil to spatter. Then stir to evenly coat everything with oil, a few seconds.

Add the shallot to the wok and fry over medium heat until softened, less than a minute. Add the dill, ¼ teaspoon of the salt, and a couple tablespoons of water. Turn the heat to medium-low, cover, and cook for 10 to 15 minutes. Stir from time to time. When cooked, the dill should be darker in color and not have as strong a flavor as raw dill. Add the vangi baath powder. Fry for another minute.

Stir in the cooked rice and season with ¼ to ½ teaspoon salt. Stir-fry for 1 or 2 minutes. Mix in the pistachios, reserving a few for garnish. Turn off the heat. Stir in the lime juice and garnish with the reserved pistachios. Taste for salt and lime and adjust as needed. Serve hot with raita and hot pickle.

FRAGRANT EGGPLANT AND GREEN PEPPER RICE *Vangi Baath*

Ⓥ Ⓖ Summer, Fall • Serves 4

Vangi baath, which translates to "mixed eggplant and rice," is a classic South Indian dish made with a fragrant spice powder of roasted dals, coriander seeds, cinnamon, cloves, and red chiles. I use the spice blend often to flavor roasted vegetables (page 85). You can buy the spice blend at Indian shops or online or make it yourself.

I stumbled upon the combination of eggplant, green bell pepper, and onion after receiving these three vegetables together in my farm share one year. I vary the vegetable combinations from time to time, such as using corn and edamame, and for a pop-up dinner I used farro instead of rice, which works very well. This rice pairs well with raita or majjige huli, an herby coconut yogurt curry.

I use lemon juice in my rice, but tamarind paste is the traditional way to add a sour component. Even though I don't love using a nonstick pan, I recommend it for this dish so the eggplant doesn't stick.

4 cups cooked turmeric rice (page 100 or 101); substitute jasmine rice for the basmati if you prefer*

¼ cup unsweetened grated coconut (fresh, frozen, or dried)

1 long, slender Asian or Italian eggplant

2 tablespoons plus 1½ teaspoons peanut or canola oil, or more as needed

½ teaspoon black mustard seeds

Pinch of asafetida (hing) powder

1 teaspoon chana dal

1 teaspoon urad dal

5 fresh curry leaves

1 dried red chile, broken in half

1 small red onion, chopped

¼ teaspoon turmeric powder

Salt

1 small green bell pepper, chopped

1½ tablespoons vangi baath powder, homemade (page 198) or store-bought**

Juice of half a lemon (about 1½ tablespoons), plus more as needed

2 tablespoons chopped cilantro, plus more for garnish

SERVING OPTIONS

Raita (pages 72 to 76) or coconut yogurt curry (page 69)

*Leftover rice also works well in this recipe.

**You can use huli powder (page 196) or store-bought sambar powder as a substitute.

Spread the cooked rice on a sheet pan to cool completely. Thaw frozen coconut or place dried coconut in a little hot water to plump it up.

Cut the eggplant into ½-inch-thick matchsticks, 2 inches long. Place the freshly cut eggplant into a bowl of water to prevent browning.

Coat the bottom of a wok or large frying pan with 2 tablespoons of the oil and place over medium heat. When the oil is hot and shimmering, add one black mustard seed. When the seed sizzles and pops, add the rest of the mustard seeds and the asafetida. Keep a lid handy to cover the pan while the mustard seeds are popping. When the popping starts to subside (a few seconds), immediately add the chana dal and urad dal. Stir to coat with oil, and turn the heat to medium-low. Continue to stir the dals so they evenly roast, until they turn a reddish golden brown and smell nutty, less than a minute. Rub the curry leaves between your fingers a little to release their natural oils, and drop them and the dried red chile into the oil. Cover immediately, as moisture from the curry leaves will cause the oil to spatter. Then stir to evenly coat everything with oil, a few seconds.

Add the onion and turmeric powder to the wok and fry until softened and translucent, a couple of minutes. Drain the eggplant and add to the wok with a sprinkling of salt and mix well. Fry for 1 minute and then add the bell pepper. Fry for 1 minute more. Over medium-high heat, stir-fry until the eggplant is almost cooked through but still holds its shape, 3 to 4 minutes. If the pan is getting dry, add a bit more oil.

Clear a little space in the middle of the pan. Add the remaining 1½ teaspoons oil and the vangi baath powder. Mix the powder and oil well, and let it fry for a few seconds. Then mix the eggplant well with the oil and stir-fry until the eggplant is cooked through but still holds its shape, a couple of minutes longer.

When the eggplant is cooked, stir in the cooked rice and ½ teaspoon salt and mix well to distribute the spices. Stir in the coconut and fry for another minute. Turn off the heat.

Mix in the lemon juice and cilantro. Taste for salt and lemon and adjust if needed. Garnish with more chopped cilantro. Serve hot, plain or with raita.

COCONUT RICE WITH CASHEWS *Kayi Anna*

V G All seasons • Serves 4

This rice is a celebration of coconut, which is an auspicious ingredient in South India, often used in Hindu religious ceremonies or pujas. Coconuts are cracked open and offered up to the gods during momentous occasions, like a new home purchase or a child graduating from college.

To enhance the coconut flavor even further, I cook the rice and fry the cashews in coconut oil. When in season, I change up the traditional recipe and add pomegranate seeds or red currants for their tart sweetness. This rice is perfect plain and great to carry on a picnic or to a potluck.

4 cups cooked turmeric rice (page 100 or 101); substitute jasmine rice for the basmati if you prefer*

1 cup unsweetened grated coconut (fresh, frozen, or dried)

2 tablespoons plus ½ teaspoon coconut oil

2 tablespoons cashews, broken into large pieces

½ teaspoon black mustard seeds

Pinch of asafetida (hing) powder

1 teaspoon urad dal

4 or 5 fresh curry leaves

1 dried red chile, broken in half

½ to ¾ teaspoon salt

¼ cup pomegranate seeds or fresh red currants (optional)

Chopped cilantro leaves, for garnish

*Leftover rice also works well in this recipe.

Spread the cooked rice on a sheet pan to cool completely. Thaw frozen coconut or place dried coconut in a little hot water to plump it up.

Melt ½ teaspoon of the coconut oil in a wok or sauté pan over medium heat. Add the cashews to the wok, stirring them until they are fragrant and turn golden brown, a few minutes. Set the cashews aside to cool in a bowl lined with a paper towel.

Coat the bottom of the wok or a large frying pan with the remaining 2 tablespoons of coconut oil and place over medium heat. When melted, add one black mustard seed. When the seed sizzles and pops, add the rest of the mustard seeds and the asafetida. Keep a lid handy to cover the pan while the mustard seeds are popping. When the popping starts to subside (a few seconds), immediately add the urad dal. Stir to coat with oil, and turn the heat to medium-low. Continue to stir the dal so it evenly roasts, until it turns a reddish golden brown and smells nutty, less than a minute. Rub the curry leaves between your fingers a little to release their natural oils, and drop them and the dried red chile into the oil. Cover immediately, as moisture from the curry leaves will cause the oil to spatter. Then stir to evenly coat everything with oil, a few seconds.

Stir the cooked rice into the wok, coating it well with the oil and spices. Mix in the coconut and ½ teaspoon of the salt. Stir-fry for a few minutes. Mix in the pomegranate seeds and cashews, reserving a few cashews for garnish. Turn off the heat. Taste for salt and adjust if needed. Garnish with the cilantro and reserved cashews before serving.

YOGURT RICE WITH POMEGRANATE AND MINT *Mosaranna*

G All seasons • Serves 4

Mosaranna, which means "yogurt rice" or "curd rice," is a staple in South Indian homes. It's white, fluffy, and cooling–I compare it to eating clouds. I have a special place in my heart for yogurt rice. From a young age, I would mix plain rice, yogurt, and a little salt or hot pickle together on my plate, relishing each bite just as much as I do today.

This recipe for yogurt rice is based on the version my mother would make for picnics or when we'd have guests over. It's spruced up with fried spices, chile, and curry leaves. I have included pomegranate seeds, which add a nice burst of color and some sweetness. Other additions that work are halved grapes, green peas, fried nuts, and shredded coconut. Fresh dill or cilantro can be used in place of the mint in this recipe.

4 cups cooked turmeric rice (page 100 or 101); substitute jasmine rice for the basmati if you prefer*

1½ cups plain whole-milk yogurt, beaten by hand, plus more as needed

¼ cup sour cream

½ teaspoon salt

2 teaspoons mild-flavored oil such as canola

½ teaspoon black mustard seeds

Pinch of asafetida (hing) powder

½ teaspoon chana dal

½ teaspoon urad dal

4 or 5 fresh curry leaves

1 or 2 Indian green chiles or serrano chiles, finely chopped

Buttermilk, plain kefir, or milk (optional)

¼ cup pomegranate seeds, plus more for garnish

1 tablespoon chopped mint leaves, plus more for garnish

Hot pickle (pages 185 to 189) or Brooklyn Delhi achaar, for serving (opional)

*Leftover rice also works well in this recipe.

Spread the cooked rice on a sheet pan to cool to room temperature.

In a large bowl, combine the cooled rice, yogurt, sour cream, and salt.

Put the oil in a tempering pot or small pan over medium heat. When the oil is hot and shimmering, add one black mustard seed. When the seed sizzles and pops, add the rest of the mustard seeds and the asafetida. Keep a lid handy to cover the pan while the mustard seeds are popping. When the popping starts to subside (a few seconds), immediately add the chana dal and urad dal. Stir to coat with oil, and turn the heat to medium-low. Continue to stir the dals so they evenly roast, until they turn a reddish golden brown and smell nutty, less than a minute. Rub the curry leaves between your fingers a little to release their natural oils, and drop them and the green chile into the oil. Cover immediately, as moisture from the curry leaves will cause the oil to spatter. Then stir to evenly coat everything with oil, and continue to fry until the chile is less raw, 10 to 15 seconds. Turn off the heat.

Immediately pour the oil mixture over the yogurt rice. To get all of the oil out of the pan, put a spoonful or two of the rice into the pan, stir, and spoon it back into the bowl.

Mix all together and add more yogurt to your taste, or add a bit of buttermilk, kefir, or milk if you want a looser consistency. Gently mix in the pomegranate seeds and chopped mint. Taste for salt and adjust as needed. Garnish with the mint and pomegranate seeds. Serve plain or with hot pickle.

YELLOW LENTIL AND RICE "RISOTTO"
Khara Huggi or *Pongal*

Ⓖ All seasons • Serves 4

Fittingly named, huggi is the ultimate comfort food. You definitely feel like you're being hugged when eating it. It's made from rice, yellow lentils called moong dal, which are split mung beans without skin, and black pepper and cumin seeds fried in ghee or butter. The lentils and rice cook together, making a creamy, rich dish resembling risotto. Traditionally, this dish is served with additional melted butter or ghee on top. I usually pair it with tangy accompaniments, like raitas, my green beans palya, cilantro coconut chutney, Brooklyn Delhi tomato achaar, or even a dash of lemon juice. Feel free to substitute red lentils for the yellow variety if that's what you have on hand.

Similar rice and lentil dishes exist throughout India, and are known by different names. This rice dish is also known as pongal in South India and is often served during the Hindu harvest festival of Sankranthi. There are spicy and sweet versions. You can make the sweet version by omitting the black pepper, cumin, asafetida, and ginger and adding sugar, golden raisins, and ground cardamom.

1 cup basmati rice, preferably Dehraduni, or jasmine rice

⅓ cup moong dal or red lentils

¼ teaspoon turmeric powder

4 tablespoons plus ½ teaspoon ghee (page 202) or unsalted butter

1 teaspoon peeled, grated fresh ginger

2 tablespoons cashews, broken into large pieces

1 teaspoon cumin seeds or ground cumin

½ teaspoon whole black peppercorns or freshly ground black pepper

1¼ teaspoons salt

¼ cup dried unsweetened shredded coconut

Big pinch of asafetida (hing) powder

Wash the rice in several changes of water until the water runs clear. Soak the rice in water, generously covered, for at least 30 minutes. (This is optional but results in softer, more evenly cooked rice.) Drain thoroughly using a fine-mesh sieve.

In a soup pot, dry-roast and stir the lentils continuously over medium heat until they are golden brown and have a nutty aroma, 2 to 3 minutes. (This step is optional but reduces the stickiness of the dal.) Thoroughly wash the lentils using a fine-mesh colander. Return them to the pot, together with the rice, and add 3½ cups of water. Bring to a boil. Skim the foam off the top. Add the turmeric powder, 2 tablespoons of the ghee, and the ginger to the boiling mixture.

Cover and cook over low heat until the rice and lentils are completely cooked, about 20 minutes. At this point, the grains will look separate. Add another ½ cup of water and continue to cook over

continued

YELLOW LENTIL AND RICE "RISOTTO" *continued*

medium-low heat, partially covered, for about 5 minutes. When you stir the mixture, it should have a creamy consistency. Feel free to mash the rice and lentils with a spoon. The consistency should be similar to a risotto. Turn off the heat.

While the rice and lentils are cooking, put ½ teaspoon of the ghee in a tempering pot or small pan over medium heat. Add the cashews, stirring them until they are fragrant and turn golden brown, a few minutes. Set the cashews aside to cool in a bowl lined with a paper towel. If using cumin seeds and peppercorns, roughly crush them in a mortar with a pestle. Set aside.

When the rice and lentil mixture is cooked, mix in the salt, coconut, and fried cashews, reserving some cashews for garnish.

Put the remaining 2 tablespoons of ghee in the tempering pot or small pan over medium heat. When melted, add the crushed black peppercorns and cumin seeds and the asafetida. Fry for a few seconds until fragrant. Turn off the heat.

Immediately pour the spiced ghee over the rice. To get all of the spiced ghee out of the pot, put a spoonful of the rice mixture into the pot, stir, and spoon it back into the rest of the dish. Taste for salt and adjust as needed. Garnish with the reserved cashews. Serve hot.

When reheating, add a little water to loosen up the dish, as it has a tendency to dry out.

THIN FLATBREAD *Chapati or Roti*

All seasons • Makes 6 chapatis

Chapati is the everyday bread of North India. The flatbread is made with atta, or durum wheat flour. To eat chapatis, you pull a little piece off with one hand and encase a bit of curry or lentils in it before putting it in your mouth. When I was younger, my paternal grandmother used to put curry in the middle of my chapati and roll it up like a burrito for me. My father, who is from northern India, is the designated chapati maker in our family, and this is his recipe. Serve chapatis with thovvay (page 139) or a vegetable dish (pages 80 to 97). To learn more about tools for making chapati, see page 35.

1 cup chapati flour or atta, plus more for rolling*	Ghee (page 202)or unsalted butter, for finishing
About ½ cup lukewarm water	

*You can substitute a mixture of whole wheat flour and all-purpose flour.

Sift the flour into a bowl, and slowly add the water while kneading to get a dough that is soft, smooth, and pliable. The longer you knead the dough the better, but 5 minutes of heavy kneading will do.

Cover the dough ball with a damp cloth and let it rest for a minimum of 30 minutes. (You can also store it in the refrigerator for making chapatis another day.) Knead the dough again for less than a minute. Divide the dough into 6 pieces and form

into balls. Line a plate with a layer of flour and roll each ball in flour. Take 1 ball of dough and flatten it down between your palms. Flour both sides of the flattened dough using the flour in the plate. Use a rolling pin to roll out the ball to a 6-inch diameter, flipping it over and dipping it into the plate of flour as needed so it does not stick.

Heat a tava (see page 35) or heavy skillet over medium heat. When it is hot (water drops should sizzle immediately), brush dry flour off both sides of the rolled chapati with your hand and place it on the skillet. When you start to see bubbles form in many places, about 20 seconds, flip the chapati over and cook until the other side does the same, about 20 seconds longer. There will just be a couple small brown spots, but mainly little bubbles.

If you are using a gas stove, turn the adjacent burner to a medium-high flame. With flat metal tongs, place the chapati straight on the flame until it puffs up, turning it on the flame to evenly cook it all around and on its edges. Turn off the flame. If you are cooking on an electric or induction stove, press the chapati in different places with a cloth to make it puff up a bit right in the skillet.

Brush off any excess flour on the chapati. Brush one side with melted ghee and place in an airtight container lined with paper towels.

Repeat with the remaining dough balls, adjusting the burner to maintain the heat of the skillet. I usually turn the heat to medium-low under the skillet while I roll the next chapati. Serve hot.

SPICY SWEET POTATO BUNS *Khara Buns*

Fall, Winter • Makes 16 small buns or 12 medium buns

Bangalore bakeries are mostly run by Iyengars, a Brahmin community known for their inventive eggless baked goods. The first of these bakeries, called Iyengar Bangalore Bakery, or BB for short, started out as a sweet shop more than a century ago and soon moved into baked goods after the owner learned from an English patron how to bake bread. Our family would often purchase special baked goods from these bakeries, like khara buns, small, spicy yeasted buns flavored with green chiles, cilantro, browned onions, and cumin seeds.

Here is my riff on khara buns using sweet potato and scallions. Traditionally, these are shaped like hamburger buns and consumed as a snack with tea or coffee. Ben and I enjoy them for breakfast filled with an egg over easy, sharp Cheddar, cabbage kosambri slaw (page 62), and Brooklyn Delhi tomato achaar.

1 large sweet potato
or yam

½ cup warm water
(110° to 115°F)

2¼ teaspoons or 1 packet
active dry yeast

1½ tablespoons sugar

5 or 6 scallions

3 tablespoons unsalted
butter, melted, plus more
for brushing tops

½ cup chopped cilantro
leaves

2 or 3 Indian green chiles
or serrano chiles, finely
chopped

½ teaspoon red chile
powder, cayenne pepper,
or dried chile flakes

1½ teaspoons salt

3 to 3½ cups all-purpose
flour, plus more for dusting

Fleur de sel, for sprinkling

Preheat the oven to 400°F. Prick the sweet potato with a fork in a few spots. Wrap it in foil and bake until tender to the prick of a fork, about 50 minutes. Peel the skin off and mash the sweet potato. You'll get about 1 cup. Let cool. (You can do this a day ahead.)

In a large bowl, whisk the warm water with the yeast and sugar until combined. Let stand for 5 minutes, or until the yeast begins to foam.

Finely chop the white and green parts of the scallions. You will end up with about ¾ cup.

Add the cooled mashed sweet potato, scallions, melted butter, cilantro, green chiles, red chile powder, and salt to the foamy yeast mixture. Stir the mixture together, using a wooden spoon. Mix in 3 cups of the flour, 1 cup at a time, until it is well combined and the dough starts pulling away from the sides of the bowl.

Turn the dough out onto a floured surface and knead, adding more flour as needed to keep the dough from sticking to the surface. Knead until the dough is soft, smooth, springy, somewhat elastic, and slightly tacky to the touch. Shape the dough into a ball.

Grease a large bowl with oil. Place the dough ball in the bowl and roll it around so it is lightly coated with the oil. Cover with clear plastic wrap. Place it in a warm corner of your kitchen until it doubles in size, 1 to 2 hours.

Grease a rimmed baking sheet, or line it with parchment paper. Turn the dough out onto a lightly floured surface and punch it down flat. Then shape it into a rectangle about ¾ inch thick. Using a dough scraper or pizza cutter, cut the dough into 12 to 16 pieces, depending on how large you want the buns to be. Roll each piece into a smooth ball, using a touch of flour if the dough is sticking. Place each ball on the prepared baking sheet, spacing them 2 to 3 inches apart so they can expand freely. Cover the buns loosely with clear plastic wrap and let them rise in a warm corner of your kitchen until they double in size, about 1 hour.

Preheat the oven to 400°F. Place the buns in the oven and bake until they are browned on top and bottom, about 15 minutes, rotating the pan halfway through.

Take the buns out of the oven and immediately brush the tops with melted butter and sprinkle of fleur de sel. Serve warm.

Refrigerate any leftover buns and heat them up in the oven or toaster before serving.

GREEN CHILE AND HERBED CHEDDAR SHORTBREAD

Masala Biscuit

All seasons • Makes about 16 biscuits

Masala biscuits, sometimes called khara biscuits, are another treat, besides the buns mentioned on page 116, that we'd get at Iyengar bakeries. They are fashioned after British biscuits, which are more like thick crackers, similar in shape and texture to a savory shortbread.

We had received a parcel of local Wisconsin cheeses from Ben's mother when I concocted this recipe. It's a perfect mix of tangy Cheddar and yogurt, herby curry leaves, cilantro, and spicy green chiles. The best part is that you can mix all of the ingredients together in a bowl by hand, without using a mixer or food processor. Because of my tiny New York kitchen, I'm a big advocate of cutting down on vessels when I can.

Feel free to substitute other herbs for the curry leaves in this recipe. These are the type of snack we'd devour with hot filter coffee (page 175) in the afternoons at my grandmother's house.

In a mixing bowl, cream the butter and sugar together by hand. Mix in the yogurt until well combined. Mix in the salt, green chiles, cilantro, and curry leaves. Mix in the flour and Cheddar until well blended.

Start gathering the ingredients together with your hands until you form a dough. It will feel quite loose in the beginning, but will firm up within a minute of kneading the ingredients together with your palms. Handle the dough as little as possible after you have brought it together.

Roll the dough into a cylinder with a diameter of 1½ inches. Wrap it in clear plastic wrap and chill in the refrigerator for 1 hour.

Preheat the oven to 350°F. Grease a rimmed baking sheet or line with parchment paper.

When ready to bake, cut ¼-inch-thick disks from the dough cylinder. Place the disks on the prepared baking sheet and bake for 18 to 20 minutes, rotating the sheet halfway through. The shortbread should be browned on the bottom and have golden spots from the Cheddar on top.

Sprinkle with fleur de sel, if desired. Serve warm.

The biscuits can be stored in an airtight container for up to 3 days.

¼ cup unsalted butter, at room temperature

1½ teaspoons sugar

2 tablespoons plain yogurt

½ teaspoon kosher salt

1 or 2 Indian green chiles or serrano chiles, finely chopped

¼ cup chopped cilantro leaves

10 fresh curry leaves, chopped

1 cup all-purpose flour

1 cup grated sharp Cheddar cheese

Fleur de sel, for sprinkling (optional)

5

SOUPS, STEWS, AND LENTILS

Lentils, or bele in Kannada and dal in Hindi, are central to Indian cooking and have been the main source of protein for vegetarians in India for centuries. India grows a quarter of all of the lentils in the world. They are everpresent on the plate and, in South India, are almost always paired with rice and yogurt to make a complete meal, rich in fiber and iron.

Since lentils play such a large role in the diet, there are a myriad of inventive preparations associated with them, from cooking in liquid, fermenting, and frying to germinating and steaming. To top it off, they are really cheap! I have bags and bags of different varieties of lentils that I work through each winter when seasonal produce is scarce.

The many varieties of legumes are prepared with aromatic spice blends, fresh vegetables and herbs, tamarind, and coconut. I devote the majority of this chapter to variations on saaru and huli, staples in the South Indian home. They are my comfort food and what I make on a rainy day or crave when I need a good, hearty bowl of home.

BASIC TOOR DAL

Ⓥ Ⓖ All seasons • Serves 4

Toor dal, also referred to as split pigeon peas, is the lentil cooked most often in Karnataka homes.

This recipe and the one on the facing page are referenced in this chapter quite a bit. I recommend bookmarking them. To save time, you can cook a large pot of these lentils, refrigerate or freeze them, and then take out portions for quickly making one of the recipes that follow.

If it's a busy night, I sometimes will eat plain lentils as is, piling on a palya (pages 80 to 82) or stir-fry dish, a dollop of yogurt, and some hot Indian pickle (pages 185 to 189) or Brooklyn Delhi achaar. If I have some cooked rice or grains, that's a bonus!

1 cup toor dal

4 cups water

¼ teaspoon turmeric powder

¾ to 1 teaspoon salt

Wash the toor dal thoroughly, using a fine-mesh colander.

Soak the dal for 1 hour or more in hot water (you can soak it overnight or in the morning before work). Drain the dal.

Add the dal to a saucepan with the 4 cups water. Bring to a boil. Stay by the stove and monitor the foaming, as your pot could quickly boil over if you are not watching. Skim off the foam. Mix in the turmeric powder. Turn the heat down to medium-low, partially cover, and simmer until the lentils are cooked through, 45 minutes to 1 hour. The toor dal should be soft and creamy when done. Cooking time does vary for this dal, depending on how old the lentils are.

Mix in ¾ teaspoon of the salt, adding a little more if necessary after tasting, and optionally mash the dal with a spoon or puree with an immersion blender to make a smooth mixture.

BASIC RED LENTILS

V G All seasons • Serves 4

Red lentils, referred to as masoor dal in Hindi, are less traditional in South Indian cooking but can be used as a substitute for toor dal. These lentils are more readily available in grocery stores and take less time to cook.

1 cup red lentils
(masoor dal)

4 cups water

¼ teaspoon turmeric
powder

¾ to 1 teaspoon salt

Wash the red lentils thoroughly, using a fine-mesh colander.

Add the lentils to a saucepan with the water. Bring to a boil. Stay by the stove and monitor the foaming, as your pot could quickly boil over if you are not watching. Skim off the foam. Mix in the turmeric powder. Turn the heat down to medium-low, partially cover, and simmer until cooked through, about 25 minutes.

Mix in ¾ teaspoon of the salt, adding a little more if necessary after tasting, and optionally mash the lentils with a spoon or puree with an immersion blender to make a smooth mixture.

SPICY AND SOUR TOMATO LENTIL SOUP
Tomato Bele Saaru or Rasam

 Ⓥ Ⓖ Summer, Fall • Serves 4

Saaru is a spicy and tangy lentil soup served plain or with rice in Karnataka homes daily. Similar soups are prepared throughout South India and are also referred to as rasam or chaaru. The saaru I grew up eating most often is made with tomatoes and an intoxicating spice blend called saarina pudi, which you can make at home or buy in Indian shops, where it will be labeled as rasam powder. Each household has its own way of preparing the dish. For instance, my mother flavors hers with cumin seeds, while my Auntie Shantha uses black mustard seeds and a pinch of cinnamon powder. I personally like all three seasonings!

When I was growing up, my mom would buy tomatoes from a local farm stand to make saaru and I'd eat a couple whole right there just like fruit, juice dripping down my chin. Tomatoes at the height of the season—heirlooms if I'm lucky enough to have them—are phenomenal in this recipe. The rest of the year, I use diced canned San Marzanos.

In our family, the most popular way to eat saaru is mixed with rice (also referred to as anna saaru), and green beans palya, sometimes with plain yogurt and lemon pickle as well. And this is a little secret, but on special occasions we would enjoy our anna saaru topped with crushed potato chips. Saaru is also enjoyed as a plain soup.

Basic toor dal (page 122) or basic red lentils (page 123), with a handful of chopped cilantro stalks or a sprig of curry leaves added during cooking

4 medium-size tomatoes (1 pound), diced, or 1 (14.5-ounce) can diced tomatoes

2 teaspoons saaru powder (page 194) or store-bought rasam powder

½ teaspoon salt

3 cups water, plus more as needed

1 teaspoon granulated jaggery or brown sugar

1 teaspoon tamarind paste

1 tablespoon ghee (page 202), unsalted butter, or canola oil

½ teaspoon black mustard seeds

Pinch of asafetida (hing) powder

½ teaspoon cumin seeds

Pinch of ground cinnamon

2 or 3 fresh curry leaves

Chopped cilantro leaves, for garnish

SERVING OPTIONS

Cooked rice (pages 100 to 101)

Green bean and coconut stir-fry (page 82)

Plain yogurt

Meyer lemon pickle (page 185) or Brooklyn Delhi rhubarb ginger achaar

Have the cooked dal ready.

In a soup pot, combine the tomatoes, saaru powder, salt, and 1 cup of the water. Bring to a boil and cook over medium-high heat for 5 minutes. Make sure the saaru powder has dissolved well; you can use a whisk or egg beater. You should start to see a golden residue forming on the top of the boiling soup. Add the jaggery and tamarind paste.

When the soup is red in color and the tomatoes are falling apart, add the cooked dal to the pot. Add the remaining 2 cups of water to the pot. Bring to a boil, then continue to simmer for 10 minutes.

continued

SPICY AND SOUR TOMATO LENTIL SOUP *continued*

During this time, adjust the water quantity to your preference. Taste for sourness and add more tamarind paste if needed. If adding more tamarind, boil the saaru a couple more minutes for the flavors to meld. Traditionally, this recipe has a thin broth on top with the cooked dal resting on the bottom of the pot. Taste the saaru; it should taste sour, spicy, sweet, and salty. Turn off the heat.

Put the ghee in a tempering pot or small pan over medium heat. When melted, add one black mustard seed. When the seed sizzles and pops, add the rest of the mustard seeds and the asafetida. Keep a lid handy to cover the pan while the mustard seeds are popping. When the popping starts to subside (a few seconds), stir in the cumin seeds and cinnamon. When the seeds turn a darker shade of brown (a few seconds), turn the heat to medium-low. Rub the curry leaves between your fingers a little to release their natural oils, and drop them into the ghee. Cover immediately, as moisture from the curry leaves will cause the ghee to spatter. Then stir to evenly coat everything with ghee, a few seconds. Turn off the heat.

Immediately pour the spiced ghee over the saaru. To get all of the ghee out of the pan, put a spoonful or two of the saaru in the small pan, stir, and then spoon it back into the pot. Taste for salt and adjust as needed. Garnish with chopped cilantro leaves.

Serve hot with rice and green bean and coconut stir-fry, or eat plain. It also pairs well with yogurt and hot lemon pickle.

When reheating the saaru, you may have to add a bit of water, as it has a tendency to thicken up in the fridge.

LEMONY LENTIL SOUP *Nimbe Saaru or Rasam*

  All seasons • Serves 4

My mother would prepare nimbe saaru when I was feeling under the weather to give me a boost. You can't help but feel as though you're doing something very good for your body when you're eating this soup. It's packed with lemon juice, ginger, protein-rich lentils, and black pepper, which clears congestion. I don't want to label this a sick soup because it is too tasty to prepare on an infrequent basis. This is one of the lentil dishes that I make most often. Serve hot as a soup or over your grain of choice with a dollop of plain yogurt or raita (pages 72 to 76) and hot pickle (pages 185 to 189).

Basic toor dal (page 122) or basic red lentils (page 123)

4 or 5 fresh curry leaves

1-inch piece fresh ginger, peeled and grated

1 or 2 Indian green chiles or serrano chiles, stemmed and sliced lengthwise down the middle

1 to 2 cups water

1 tablespoon ghee (page 202), unsalted butter, or canola oil

½ teaspoon cumin seeds

¼ teaspoon crushed black peppercorns

Pinch of asafetida (hing) powder

Juice of 1 lemon (about 3 tablespoons)

½ teaspoon salt

Chopped cilantro leaves, for garnish

While the dal is cooking, add the curry leaves, ginger, and green chile at the same time that you add the turmeric. Add the water to the cooked dal to get to the consistency of a soup. Traditionally, this recipe has a thin broth on top with the cooked dal resting on the bottom of the pot.

Put the ghee in a tempering pot or small pan over medium heat. When melted, add one cumin seed. When the seed sizzles, add the rest of the cumin seeds along with the peppercorns and asafetida. When the cumin seeds start to turn a darker shade of brown (a few seconds), turn off the heat.

Immediately pour the spiced ghee over the dal. To get all of the ghee out of the pan, put a spoonful or two of the saaru into the pan, stir, and then spoon it back into the pot. Mix in the lemon juice and salt, taste, and adjust the salt as needed. Garnish with cilantro before serving.

When reheating the saaru, you may have to add a bit of water, as it has a tendency to thicken up in the fridge.

ROASTED KABOCHA SQUASH AND COCONUT MILK SOUP

Ⓥ Ⓖ Fall, Winter • Serves 4

Kabocha squash, sometimes called Japanese pumpkin, is one of my favorite winter vegetables. I make a beeline for it when I see it at the farmers' market. It's very creamy in texture compared to other squashes and pumpkins.

Saarina pudi, the spice mixture used to make tomato saaru, actually has quite a few warming spices that are complementary to pumpkin, like coriander seeds, cumin, fenugreek, and black pepper. Saaru is usually a fine balance of spicy, sweet, and sour, which is where the coconut milk and lime juice come in.

This is one of those recipes where you can roast the squash over the weekend and then make the saaru quickly during the week. I serve it plain or topped with cilantro and a swirl of yogurt. Feel free to substitute butternut squash or sweet potatoes for the kabocha squash.

1 small kabocha squash (2 pounds), or butternut squash or sweet potatoes

2 teaspoons mild-flavored oil such as canola

1 (13.5-ounce) can unsweetened coconut milk

2 teaspoons saaru powder (page 194) or store-bought rasam powder

1 to 2 cups vegetable broth or water

1½ tablespoons ghee (page 202), unsalted butter, or coconut oil

½ teaspoon black mustard seeds

Pinch of asafetida (hing) powder

½ teaspoon cumin seeds

1 sprig curry leaves (about 20 leaves)

Pinch of ground cinnamon

¼ teaspoon turmeric powder

1-inch piece fresh ginger, peeled and grated

1 or 2 Indian green chiles or serrano chiles

1¼ teaspoons salt

1 to 2 teaspoons jaggery or brown sugar (optional)

Juice of half a lime (about 1½ tablespoons), plus more as needed

Chopped mixed herbs such as cilantro, parsley, and basil, for garnish

SERVING OPTIONS

Cooked brown rice or farro

Plain yogurt or raita (pages 72 to 76)

Hot pickle (pages 185 to 189) or Brooklyn Delhi achaar

Preheat the oven to 400°F. Cut the kabocha squash in half and remove the seeds and stringy parts. Pour the oil onto a sheet pan and then place the squash pieces, cut sides down, on the pan. Move them around on the pan so that they are coated evenly with oil. Roast the squash until you are easily able to pierce the skin with a fork, about 45 minutes. When cooled, scoop out the inside of the squash and set aside.

In a blender, puree the roasted kabocha with the coconut milk, saaru powder, and 1 cup of the broth.

continued

ROASTED KABOCHA SQUASH AND COCONUT MILK SOUP *continued*

Put the ghee in a soup pot over medium heat. When melted, add one black mustard seed. When the seed sizzles and pops, add the rest of the mustard seeds and the asafetida. Keep a lid handy to cover the pan while the mustard seeds are popping. When the popping starts to subside (a few seconds), stir in the cumin seeds. When the seeds turn a darker shade of brown (a few seconds), turn the heat to medium-low. Rub the curry leaves between your fingers a little to release their natural oils, and drop them and the cinnamon, turmeric powder, ginger, and green chile into the ghee. Cover immediately, as moisture from the curry leaves will cause the ghee to spatter. Then stir to evenly coat everything with ghee and continue to fry until the ginger and chile are less raw, 10 to 15 seconds.

Add the contents of the blender to the pot and mix well. Add the salt and more broth to get to your desired consistency. Depending on the sweetness of the squash, add the jaggery if needed. Bring the soup to a boil and then simmer for 8 to 10 minutes. Turn off the heat. Mix the lime juice into the soup. Taste for salt and lime and adjust as needed. Garnish with mixed herbs.

Serve plain or over brown rice or farro with a dollop of plain yogurt and hot pickle.

POTATO, CARROT, AND RED LENTIL STEW
Tharakaari Huli or *Sambar*

V G All seasons • Serves 4

Huli is a spicy lentil and vegetable stew served daily in Karnataka homes, usually with rice. Similar stews are prepared throughout South India and referred to as sambar. The stew is flavored with tamarind, coconut, curry leaves, and a spice blend called huli powder, which you can make at home or buy in Indian shops, where it will be labeled as sambar powder.

You can make huli with several vegetables or just one. When I make it with mixed vegetables, my favorite combination is potato, carrot, and onion, but it works well with spinach, green beans, daikon, kohlrabi, cabbage or chayote squash.

This recipe is for my weekday, one-pot version of huli. Traditionally, the stew is made with toor dal (page 122), but I use quicker-cooking red lentils when I'm short on time.

1 cup red lentils
(masoor dal)

2 tablespoons unsweetened grated coconut (fresh, frozen, or dried)

1 tablespoon ghee, (page 202), unsalted butter, or canola oil

1 tablespoon mild-flavored oil such as canola

½ teaspoon black mustard seeds

Pinch of asafetida (hing) powder

4 or 5 fresh curry leaves

1 dried red chile, broken into pieces

½ red onion, diced

¼ teaspoon turmeric powder

1 large carrot, peeled and cut into ¼-inch-thick disks

1 medium red potato, peeled and cut into ½-inch cubes

Salt

6 cups water

2 tablespoons huli powder (page 196) or store-bought sambar powder

1 teaspoon tamarind paste, plus more as needed

Chopped cilantro leaves, for garnish

SERVING OPTIONS

Cooked rice
(pages 100 to 101)

Plain yogurt or raita
(pages 72 to 76)

Hot pickle (pages 185 to 189) or Brooklyn Delhi achaar

Dosas (pages 38 to 44) or idlis (pages 45 to 48)

Wash the red lentils thoroughly, using a fine-mesh colander.

Thaw frozen coconut or place dried coconut in a little hot water to plump it up.

Put the ghee and oil in a saucepan over medium heat. When the ghee has melted and the oil is hot and shimmering, add one black mustard seed. When the seed sizzles and pops, add the rest of the mustard seeds and the asafetida. Keep a lid handy to cover the pan while the mustard seeds are popping. When the popping starts to subside (a few

continued

seconds), turn the heat to medium-low. Rub the curry leaves between your fingers a little to release their natural oils, and drop them and the dried red chile into the oil. Cover immediately, as moisture from the curry leaves will cause the oil to spatter. Then stir to evenly coat everything with oil, a few seconds. Turn off the heat.

Add the onion and turmeric powder to the pan and fry until the onion has softened and is translucent, a couple of minutes. Mix in the carrot, potato, and a sprinkling of salt. Stir to coat with oil. Add the lentils and sauté for a couple of minutes. Add the water and bring to a boil. Ladle out any foam that comes to the surface. Then simmer over medium-low heat, partially covered, until the lentils are falling apart and the vegetables are tender; this should take 25 to 30 minutes.

Add the huli powder to the cooked lentils and vegetables and mix well. Add the tamarind paste and 1¼ teaspoons salt and bring to a boil. Cook at a boil for a couple of minutes, then turn the heat to medium-low and simmer for 8 to 10 minutes. Taste for salt and tamarind and adjust as needed. I like the consistency of my huli to be right in the middle, not too thick and not too thin. Add a bit more water or boil for longer depending on your preferred consistency. Mix in the coconut and simmer for a minute more. Turn off the heat. Garnish with cilantro leaves.

Serve hot over rice with a dollop of plain yogurt and hot pickle, or with dosas. You can also enjoy the stew plain.

When reheating huli, add water to get it back to your desired consistency, as it has a tendency to thicken up in the fridge.

ROASTED BUTTERNUT SQUASH AND LENTIL STEW
Kumbalakayi Huli or *Sambar*

V G Fall, Winter • Serves 4

When the chill of fall sets in, squash and pumpkins dominate the farmers' market with their rich hues of orange, green, and yellow. A version of huli made in South India has chunks of sweet, yellow pumpkin and is extremely creamy in texture. In place of that pumpkin, I use a roasted and pureed butternut squash. I served this to my mother when she was visiting Brooklyn one fall, and her eyes lit up. I knew then that I had something with this one.

For a quick weeknight meal, roast the squash the night before and store in the refrigerator for cooking the next night. Feel free to use other roasted squash, like kabocha or delicata, instead of the butternut squash in this recipe. This huli pairs exceptionally well with herby coconut yogurt curry, known as majjige huli, or raita.

½ recipe basic red lentils (page 123) or basic toor dal (page 122)

2 teaspoons mild-flavored oil such as canola

1 butternut squash (about 2 pounds), halved and seeds removed

2 tablespoons unsweetened grated coconut (fresh, frozen, or dried)

2 tablespoons huli powder (page 196) or store-bought sambar powder

2 to 4 cups water

1 teaspoon salt

1½ tablespoons ghee (page 202), unsalted butter, or canola oil

½ teaspoon black mustard seeds

Pinch of asafetida (hing) powder

4 or 5 fresh curry leaves

1 dried red chile, broken in half

1 scallion, both green and white parts, separated and chopped

1 tablespoon jaggery or brown sugar (optional)

Juice of half a lemon (about 1½ tablespoons), plus more as needed

Chopped cilantro leaves, for garnish

SERVING OPTIONS

Plain yogurt

Cooked rice (pages 100 to 101)

Coconut yogurt curry (page 95)

Raita (pages 72 to 76)

Prepare the red lentils and set aside.

Preheat the oven to 400°F. Pour the oil onto a sheet pan and then place the squash pieces, cut sides down, on the pan. Move them around on the pan so that they are coated evenly with oil. Roast the squash until you are easily able to pierce the skin with a fork, about 45 minutes. You can choose to use the skin of the squash if it is tender or scoop out the inside of the squash and set aside.

Thaw frozen coconut or place dried coconut in a little hot water to plump it up.

In a blender, combine the huli powder and coconut. Blend to a smooth paste with some texture from the grated coconut, adding just enough of the water (about ½ cup) to get the blender blades going, depending on how large your blender container is. Add the cooled lentils, roasted squash, and salt. Add another 1 to 2 cups of the water and puree.

Put the ghee in a saucepan over medium heat. When melted, add one black mustard seed. When the seed sizzles and pops, add the rest of the mustard seeds and the asafetida. Keep a lid handy to cover the pan while the mustard seeds are popping. When the popping starts to subside (a few seconds), turn the heat to medium-low. Rub the curry leaves between your fingers a little to release their natural oils, and drop them and the dried red chile into the ghee. Cover immediately, as moisture from the curry leaves will cause the ghee to spatter. Then stir to evenly coat everything with ghee, a few seconds. Add the white parts of the scallion to the pan and stir-fry until soft, a couple of minutes.

Add the contents of the blender to the saucepan and mix well. Add enough of the remaining water to get to your desired consistency. I like the consistency of my huli to be right in the middle, not too thick and not too thin. Add jaggery if needed, depending on how sweet your squash is. Boil the soup for a couple of minutes and then turn the heat to medium-low and simmer for 8 to 10 minutes. Turn off the heat. Mix in the lemon juice. Taste for salt and lemon juice and adjust as needed. Garnish with the green parts of the scallion and the chopped cilantro.

Serve plain or over rice, with a dollop of yogurt, curry, or raita.

When reheating huli, add water to get it back to your desired consistency, as it has a tendency to thicken up in the fridge.

BLACK-EYED PEAS, GREENS, AND LENTIL STEW

Alasande Kallu Soppina Huli or *Sambar*

Ⓥ Ⓖ All seasons • Serves 4

Huli made with black-eyed peas is a classic preparation in South India. Usually the dish also has either some kind of green, such as amaranth leaves, or cooked eggplant. I like to serve this dish when I'm catering vegetarian menus because it is protein-rich. You can substitute frozen or canned black-eyed peas for the dried ones that you will need to soak overnight before cooking. If using frozen or canned black-eyed peas, skip the soaking step.

Although amaranth leaves are technically in season in summer and into fall, I have labeled this recipe good for all seasons because you can just use spinach, kale, or other greens of your choice. I highly recommend seeking out amaranth at your local farmers' market or purchasing it from an Indian or Asian market. Its leaves are green and usually marked with a beautiful deep reddish purple coloring in the middle. The plant is also highly nutritious, full of vitamins and minerals.

For a quick variation I will sometimes prepare this recipe without the black-eyed peas and with just greens I have on hand.

½ cup dried black-eyed peas, or 1½ cups frozen or canned black-eyed peas

4 cups water

2 tablespoons unsweetened grated coconut (fresh, frozen, or dried)

Basic red lentils (page 123) or basic toor dal (page 122)

2 tablespoons huli powder (page 196) or store-bought sambar powder

1 teaspoon tamarind paste

1½ teaspoons salt

2 cups chopped amaranth leaves (callaloo), spinach, or other greens

2 tablespoons ghee (page 202), unsalted butter, or canola oil

½ teaspoon black mustard seeds

Pinch of asafetida (hing) powder

4 or 5 fresh curry leaves

1 dried red chile, broken in half

1 medium yellow onion, diced

Chopped cilantro leaves, for garnish

SERVING OPTIONS

Cooked rice (pages 100 to 101)

Plain yogurt or raita (pages 72 to 76)

Hot pickle (pages 185 to 189) or Brooklyn Delhi achaar

Rinse and soak the dried black-eyed peas overnight. The next day, drain and place in a saucepan with 2 cups of the water and bring to a boil. Skim off any foam that appears on the top. Then turn the heat down to medium-low and simmer, partially covered, until tender, 50 to 60 minutes. Check on them from time to time while cooking to make sure the beans are always covered with water.

Thaw frozen coconut or place dried coconut in a little hot water to plump it up.

Add the remaining 2 cups of water to the cooked red lentils. Add the huli powder and mix well. Add the tamarind paste and 1 teaspoon of the salt

continued

BLACK-EYED PEAS, GREENS, AND LENTIL STEW *continued*

and bring to a boil. Cook at a boil for a couple of minutes, then turn the heat to medium-low and simmer for 8 to 10 minutes. I like the consistency of my huli to be right in the middle, not too thick and not too thin. Add a bit more water or boil for longer depending on your preferred consistency. Halfway through simmering, add the black-eyed peas, amaranth leaves, and remaining ½ teaspoon of salt. Mix in the coconut and simmer for a minute more. Turn off the heat.

Put the ghee in a small frying pan or sauté pan over medium heat. When melted, add one black mustard seed. When the seed sizzles and pops, add the rest of the mustard seeds and the asafetida. Keep a lid handy to cover the pan while the mustard seeds are popping. When the popping starts to subside (a few seconds), turn the heat to medium-low. Rub the curry leaves between your fingers a little to release their natural oils, and drop them and the dried red chile into the ghee. Cover immediately, as moisture from the curry leaves will cause the ghee to spatter. Then stir to evenly coat everything with ghee, a few seconds. Add the onion and fry over medium heat until it is softened and translucent, a couple of minutes.

Immediately pour the fried onion and spices over the huli. To get all of the ghee out of the pan, put a spoonful or two of the huli into the pan, stir, and then spoon it back into the pot. Mix and taste for salt, adjusting if needed. Garnish with chopped cilantro.

Serve hot over rice with a dollop of plain yogurt or raita and hot pickle. You can also enjoy the stew plain.

When reheating huli, add water to get it back to your desired consistency, as it has a tendency to thicken up in the fridge.

CREAMY YELLOW LENTILS WITH TOMATO AND GINGER *Hesaru Bele Thovvay*

 V G All seasons • Serves 4

Thovvay is made with yellow lentils called moong dal or split mung beans without skin, the same lentils that are soaked and used in kosambri salad (page 61). The dal is flavored with ginger, curry leaves, green chiles, turmeric, and lemon. It is thick in consistency and usually served with chapatis for scooping. My Auntie Asha gave me the tip of roasting the lentils beforehand so they are less sticky to cook with.

Members of my family who adhere to the Brahmin tradition of avoiding alliums in cooking do not include shallots or garlic in this recipe, but I have added them because I like the flavor combination.

Some versions of this soup include a couple of tablespoons of shredded coconut. You can also add different vegetables to the mix if you have them on hand, such as watery squashes like zucchini, winter squash like butternut, greens like spinach, or root vegetables like beets. Feel free to substitute red lentils or toor dal for the moong dal, or to make it thinner in consistency for serving over rice.

1 cup moong dal

4 cups water

1 sprig curry leaves (about 20 leaves)

1-inch piece fresh ginger, peeled and grated

2 to 3 Indian green chiles or serrano chiles, finely chopped

¼ teaspoon turmeric powder

1 to 1¼ teaspoons salt

1 tablespoon ghee (page 202) unsalted butter, or canola oil

½ teaspoon black mustard seeds

Pinch of asafetida (hing) powder

½ teaspoon urad dal

1 shallot or ¼ red onion, chopped

1 clove garlic, minced

1 medium tomato, chopped

Juice of half a lemon (about 1½ tablespoons), plus more as needed

2 tablespoons chopped cilantro leaves, plus more for garnish

SERVING OPTIONS

Chapatis (page 115) or other flatbread

Cooked rice (pages 100 to 101)

Raita (pages 72 to 76) or plain yogurt

Dry-roast the moong dal in a saucepan over medium heat until they are golden brown and have a nutty aroma, 2 to 3 minutes. (This step is optional but reduces the stickiness of the dal.) Thoroughly wash the moong dal, using a fine-mesh colander.

Combine the moong dal and water in a saucepan. Bring to a boil. Skim the foam off the top. Mix in half of the curry leaves and the ginger, 1 or 2 green chiles, and the turmeric powder. Simmer, partially covered, over medium-low heat until cooked, about 30 minutes. The dal should be easily mashable and creamy in texture. Season with ¾ to 1 teaspoon of the salt. Turn off the heat.

continued

SOUPS, STEWS, AND LENTILS

Put the ghee in a small frying pan or sauté pan over medium heat. When melted, add one black mustard seed. When the seed sizzles and pops, add the rest of the mustard seeds and the asafetida. Keep a lid handy to cover the pan while the mustard seeds are popping. When the popping starts to subside (a few seconds), immediately add the urad dal. Stir to coat with oil, and turn the heat to medium-low. Continue to stir the dal so it evenly roasts, until it turns a reddish golden brown and smells nutty, less than a minute. Rub the remaining curry leaves between your fingers a little to release their natural oils, and drop them and the remaining green chile into the ghee. Cover immediately, as moisture from the curry leaves will cause the ghee to spatter. Then stir to evenly coat everything with ghee, a few seconds.

Add the shallot to the pan and fry over medium heat until softened and translucent, a couple of minutes. Next, add the garlic and fry until fragrant. Mix in the tomato and ¼ teaspoon of salt and cook until the tomato is falling apart, 4 to 5 minutes.

Pour the flavored ghee and tomatoes over the soup and mix. Let it all boil together for a minute or two. The consistency should be on the thicker side for soups, able to be scooped up in a chapati or to loosely rest on rice. Turn off the heat. Mix in the lemon juice and cilantro. Taste for salt and lemon juice and adjust if needed. Garnish with more chopped cilantro.

Serve hot with chapatis, or enjoy plain or over rice with a dollop of raita on top.

When reheating thovvay, add water to get it back to your desired consistency, as it has a tendency to thicken up in the fridge.

6

FESTIVE BITES
AND SNACKS

On festival days or when we were having company over, my mother would prepare a few special bites. I remember standing by her in our kitchen in New Jersey when I was quite young, watching her fry bondas, or potato fritters, in her cast-iron wok, which she still uses today. She would lay each piece on a paper towel to cool; and before the guests arrived, I would be allowed to "test" a few, dipping them in ketchup while still hot.

While in Bangalore, it's hard to miss the city's obsession with snacking. Outside one of the many popular food stalls or carts, it's customary to see a crowd of people overflowing onto the sidewalk and road enjoying local specialties. It is also customary to enjoy a few homemade or bakery snacks along with afternoon tea or coffee at home. I was and to this day still am amazed by the variety of these delicious and unique treats, from bitter gourd chips (page 152) to masala roasted peanuts (page 151). With each trip to Bangalore, I discover something new. This is just a sampling of what I have been lucky enough to enjoy and now prepare in my kitchen in Brooklyn.

LETTUCE "DOSA" WRAP
WITH CURRIED POTATO AND CHUTNEY

 V G All seasons • Serves 4 to 6

My fresh lettuce dosa is a nod to Asian lettuce wraps and a healthy play on the traditional dosa (page 38). I take a butter lettuce leaf, instead of the fried crepe, and top it with the traditional masala dosa potato filling and cilantro coconut chutney. The result is super-refreshing, with the crunch of the butter lettuce and the warm potato filling and spicy chutney on the inside.

I make these often as an appetizer for my pop-up dinner and catering clients. For a variation, I sometimes will make the curry with half sweet potatoes and half red potatoes. I have also served these using cut romaine lettuce leaves in place of the butter lettuce.

Prepare the potato stir-fry and cilantro coconut chutney.

Wash the butter lettuce leaves and pat them dry with a paper towel.

Fill each lettuce leaf with 2 tablespoons of potato curry and 1 teaspoon of chutney. Eat as you would a lettuce wrap.

Potato stir-fry with onion and ginger (page 80)

Cilantro coconut chutney (page 179)
1 head butter lettuce

BEN'S CURRY LEAF POPCORN

G All seasons • Serves 4; makes about 12 cups

When Ben and I first started dating, I taught him how to temper black mustard seeds, asafetida, curry leaves, and red chiles in oil to make several South Indian dishes. He took that lesson and applied it to one of his specialties, homemade popcorn. He seasons melted butter with the spices and then finishes off the popcorn with tangy nutritional yeast. We became so obsessed with his recipe that movie popcorn was no longer suitable. We would sneak brown paper bags of his homemade popcorn into the theater, and still do.

We usually buy popcorn kernels from the farmers' market, and we've even made it with popcorn on the cob that we've gotten from our farm share. To make this recipe vegan, substitute coconut oil for the butter. Before you begin the recipe, make sure to have a lid for the vessel you are using to pop your kernels. We have found a wok works best for this recipe.

2 tablespoons high-heat oil such as peanut or canola

½ cup popcorn kernels

2 to 3 tablespoons unsalted butter or coconut oil, to taste

1 teaspoon black mustard seeds

¼ teaspoon asafetida (hing) powder

½ sprig curry leaves (about 10 leaves)

½ teaspoon turmeric powder

2 dried red chiles, broken in half

Salt

3 tablespoons nutritional yeast

Put the oil in a wok or large, heavy-bottomed saucepan over medium-high heat. When the oil is hot and shimmering, add the popcorn kernels.

Swirl the pan around so the kernels get coated with the oil.

Cover the pan. Turn the heat to medium. You will hear a few kernels start to pop after 2 minutes. Shake the wok from time to time, so that the kernels get evenly popped. While the kernels are popping, keep the lid slightly ajar so some steam can escape. This will help the popcorn crisp up. When the popping starts to subside, after about 4 minutes, you will have a wok or pot full of popcorn. Turn off the heat. Transfer the popcorn to a large serving bowl.

Put the butter in the same wok over medium heat. When melted, add one black mustard seed. When the seed sizzles and pops, add the rest of the mustard seeds and the asafetida. Keep a lid handy to cover the pan while the mustard seeds are popping. When the popping starts to subside (a few seconds), turn the heat to medium-low. Rub the curry leaves between your fingers a little to release their natural oils, and drop them, the turmeric powder, and dried red chiles into the butter. Cover immediately, as moisture from the curry leaves will cause the butter to spatter. Then stir to evenly coat everything with butter, a few seconds.

Immediately pour the butter mixture over the popcorn. Add salt to taste as soon as you pour the butter, so that it sticks to the popcorn. Mix thoroughly. Add 2 tablespoons of the nutritional yeast and mix well. Then add the remaining 1 tablespoon of nutritional yeast and mix thoroughly. Serve warm.

STUFFED SHISHITO PEPPER FRITTERS *Bhajji*

V G Spring, Summer • Serves 4 to 6; makes about 20 fritters

On a visit to Bangalore, my cousin Vijay took me to VV Puram, one of the most famous local street-food scenes in the city. The market takes place in the evening, with a variety of foods from traditional specialties to creative riffs on the originals. My shishito pepper bhajjis, a battered and fried appetizer, are fashioned after the banana pepper bhajjis we ate that day. The batter is made from Indian chickpea flour, spices, and my addition of sparkling water for extra crunch.

Shishitos are Japanese peppers that appear at the farmers' market in droves and on menus in the city in late summer and early fall. They are mild for the most part (I've gotten a rogue hot one here and there). I stuff each freshly fried pepper with red cabbage and citrus coleslaw and top with a bit of cilantro coconut chutney. This combination is superb served in soft tacos. You can substitute different peppers like padrón or poblano for the shishitos in this recipe.

Red cabbage and citrus coleslaw (page 62)

Cilantro coconut chutney (page 179)

8 ounces shishito peppers (about 20 peppers), stems intact

1 cup besan gram flour (Indian chickpea flour), sifted

2 tablespoons rice flour

Big pinch of asafetida (hing) powder

About ½ teaspoon red chile powder

¼ teaspoon turmeric powder

1 teaspoon salt, plus more for sprinkling

½ teaspoon baking powder

½ to ¾ cup cold sparkling water

2 cups canola oil

Have the coleslaw and chutney ready. Set aside in the refrigerator to chill.

Make a vertical slit, 1 to 2 inches in length, on one side of each of the peppers. This will prevent them from popping in the oil. If you prefer, you can also take out the interior stems and seeds to reduce spiciness.

In a mixing bowl, whisk together the besan, rice flour, asafetida, red chile powder, turmeric powder, salt, and baking powder. Mix in the cold sparkling water, starting at ½ cup, until there are no lumps. The batter should be thick enough to coat a pepper when dipped in it, but not clumpy. Put the batter in the refrigerator to keep it cold.

Fill a deep pot or wok with the oil. Turn the heat to medium-high. Heat the oil to 350°F. To test without a thermometer, put a little piece of batter in the oil. If it rises to the top quickly, the oil is hot enough.

continued

Holding a pepper by the stem, dip it in the batter, shake off the excess batter, and put the pepper in the hot oil. Repeat for as many peppers as will comfortably fit in the pot. (If the batter is too thick, add a bit more cold sparkling water, and if it's too runny at this point, add a bit more besan or rice flour. You need the batter to stick and not drip off.)

Fry until the peppers are golden brown, 2 to 3 minutes. Flip them around from time to time with a slotted spoon to make sure they are evenly fried. Once they turn golden brown, place them on a plate lined with paper towels and sprinkle with salt. Repeat with the remaining peppers. Adjust the heat if the oil is getting too hot during this process.

When ready to serve, slit the peppers vertically just up to the stem. Stuff each with a spoonful of coleslaw and a drizzle of chutney.

These are best served hot, but you can also reheat them in a warm oven until they crisp up again or refry them for half a minute before stuffing and serving.

PAN-ROASTED MASALA PEANUTS *Congress Kadalekayi*

V G All seasons • Makes about 2 cups

Legend has it that Congress kadalekayi or peanuts got their name from being split in two. My family frequently buys these spicy, peppery, and downright addictive peanuts from Srinivasa Condiment Stores, a little snack shop in Bangalore that is always jam-packed with customers. Locals usually refer to it as Subbamma Angadi (*angadi* means "store") after its founder, Subbamma. Subbamma started selling her homemade snacks door to door as a way to support her family after her husband passed away. The business became such a hit that she opened up a storefront in 1948. Her grandson now runs the shop.

I re-created my version of Subbamma's famous peanuts back in Brooklyn, purposely using a pan-roasted method. Many Indian homes do not have ovens, so roasting occurs predominantly on the stove. This recipe is easiest when made with unsalted and roasted peanuts, but I provide directions if you have raw peanuts with skins.

2 cups roasted peanuts, unsalted and preferably without skins or raw peanuts with skins

1 sprig curry leaves (about 20 leaves)

1 tablespoon peanut or canola oil

⅛ teaspoon asafetida (hing) powder

¼ teaspoon turmeric powder

½ teaspoon freshly ground black pepper

½ teaspoon red chile powder

Salt

If using raw peanuts, put a wok or large frying pan over medium heat. When hot, add the peanuts. Roast, stirring all the while, until the skins start to crackle and you smell a nutty aroma, 2 to 3 minutes. It's all right if the peanuts have some golden brown spots, but they should not be darkened in color. Transfer the peanuts to a plate to cool. If your peanuts have skins, when cooled, rub them between your fingers to take their skins off. This step is a bit tedious. I sometimes put them into a lidded container and shake them hard. This helps to get some of the skins off as well.

In the same wok over medium heat, roast the curry leaves, stirring them until they start to curl up and become dry. Place them on top of the peanuts to cool. With your hands, crush the curry leaves on top of the peanuts.

Put the oil in the same wok over medium heat . Add the asafetida, turmeric powder, black pepper, and red chile powder. Mix the spices well and make sure they are coated with oil. The pan may look dry; that's okay. Quickly add the peanuts and crushed curry leaves. Mix them well so they are completely coated in the spice mixture. Add salt to taste. Turn down the heat to low and fry the peanuts for a minute more, turning them all the while. Turn off the heat and transfer the peanuts to a plate lined with paper towels. They will become crunchier as they cool. You can store the mixture in an airtight container for a few days.

SPICY BITTER GOURD CHIPS

Haggala Kayi Hot Chips

V G Summer, Fall • Serves 4

There are hot chip vendors scattered throughout Bangalore, all peddling different vegetable chips spiced with their secret masala mixture, but I always come back to the bitter gourd or melon variety. As a child I would shun this vegetable, but now I've come to appreciate its distinct bitter flavor.

Recently a farm in the Hudson Valley started growing Indian bitter gourds that are available to us in the summer and fall months locally. You can use either the spiky or the smooth variety in this recipe. Riper gourds are more bitter, darker green in color, and have red seeds while less-ripe gourds have a lighter green color and white seeds.

My hot chips are baked in the oven rather than being deep-fried, but they are just as crispy. They are great dipped into Greek yogurt or mixed into rice and lentils for a crunch. If you're not a bitter fan, you can substitute other thinly sliced vegetables such as delicata squash, beets, or sweet potatoes.

Thinly slice the gourds into 1/16-inch-thick disks, using a mandoline or sharp knife. Discard the seeds.

In a medium bowl, whisk together the rice flour, turmeric powder, chile powder, cumin powder, coriander powder, asafetida, and salt. Mix the lemon juice and oil into the flour mixture evenly. Add the bitter gourd slices and coat evenly with the thick batter using your hands. Marinate for 30 minutes.

Preheat the oven to 425°F. Grease a sheet pan.

Gently mix the bitter gourd slices with your hand as some of the oil may have settled on the bottom of the bowl. Place the battered gourd slices in a single layer on the prepared pan and sprinkle them with the sugar. Bake until the chips are golden brown and starting to crisp on one side, about 10 minutes. Flip the gourd chips, turn the tray 180 degrees, and then bake until the chips are browned and crisped on both sides, another 4 to 5 minutes. Keep an eye on them during this stage and take out any chips that look done. Remove the pan from the oven, the chips will crisp up more after cooling for a couple of minutes.

Serve with Greek yogurt, mayonnaise, or ketchup for dipping. Although best right after they are baked, you can store the chips in an airtight container for a few days. Just pop them in a warm oven to crisp up.

2 large bitter gourds (about 1/2 pound), trimmed

1/4 cup rice flour

1/4 teaspoon turmeric powder

1 teaspoon red chile powder or cayenne pepper, or to taste

1/2 teaspoon cumin powder

1/2 teaspoon coriander powder

Big pinch of asafetida (hing) powder

1/2 teaspoon salt

Juice of half a lemon (about 1 1/2 tablespoons)

1/4 cup mild-flavored oil such as canola

1/2 tablespoon sugar

Greek yogurt, fancy mayonnaise, or ketchup, for serving

FESTIVAL TRAIL MIX *Ellu Bella*

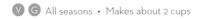

V G All seasons • Makes about 2 cups

Ellu bella is a sweet trail mix made on special holidays such as Sankranthi, a festival celebrating the harvest season. This recipe is from my mother and includes peanuts, roasted chana dal, jaggery (unrefined sugarcane), dried coconut pieces, and sesame seeds.

For this recipe, you will need jaggery in its chunk form versus granulated. You can substitute chopped blanched almonds for the roasted chana dal and panela or pilonallo for jaggery. I prefer to roast the peanuts and sesame seeds instead of purchasing them preroasted, for a fresher flavor.

I love to make a big batch and have it on hand for a healthy snack during the day. Feel free to make your own variations with dried cranberries, golden raisins, chocolate pieces, or different nuts like chopped cashews or pecans.

¼ cup unsweetened dried coconut slices

½ cup raw peanuts, preferably without skin, or unsalted roasted peanuts

¼ cup raw sesame seeds or roasted sesame seeds

½ cup roasted chana dal (chana dalia)

½ cup diced jaggery

Cut the dried coconut slices into ½-inch pieces.

If using raw peanuts and sesame seeds: Put a small frying pan or sauté pan over medium heat. When hot, add the peanuts. Roast, stirring all the while, until you smell a nutty aroma, 2 or 3 minutes. It's okay if the peanuts have some golden brown spots, but they should not be darkened in color. Transfer the peanuts to a plate to cool. Next, roast the sesame seeds in the same pan until you smell their roasted aroma and they turn golden brown, 1 to 2 minutes. Transfer the seeds to a separate plate to cool.

Combine the peanuts, sesame seeds, roasted chana dal, coconut pieces, and jaggery. You can store the mixture in an airtight container for a few weeks.

7

SWEETS AND DRINKS

Indian desserts are known for being overly rich and sweet, but luckily I grew up with parents who were fruit fanatics. Today, many of the desserts I love to prepare involve fresh fruit. On birthdays and festival days, my mother would prepare some traditional sweets that we would sample at the beginning of our meal, in accordance with South Indian custom. However, the recipes she would prepare were not too rich, and that's how I still prefer my desserts—with just enough sweetness to make you smile at the end of a good meal.

South India is coffee country. In fact, the state of Karnataka produces 70 percent of India's coffee. In Bangalore, filter or drip coffee (page 175) is a specialty, flavored with the chicory plant and paired with a generous spot of creamy milk and sugar. With the wide variety of fresh fruits in the marketplace, there is an equally impressive array of refreshing juices, which inspired my chile-watermelon juice (page 172). Some drinks also serve a medicinal purpose but are full of delicious flavor, like the herbed yogurt drink majjige (page 171) that is also a digestive.

CHIA PUDDING WITH ROASTED JAGGERY
BLUEBERRIES *Sabbakki Payasa*

 Summer • Serves 4

Payasa is a sweetened saffron milk dessert often made with either tapioca or thin noodles and usually prepared on festival days. It is the South Indian equivalent of North Indian rice pudding, or kheer. This recipe is a variation on my mother's tapioca or sabbakki payasa, using chia seeds and coconut milk. I have a number of vegan and gluten-free friends, so my chia pudding satisfies all parties. Instead of the traditional golden raisins, I top the pudding with blueberries roasted with jaggery, unrefined sugarcane.

What's great about chia seeds is that they are extraordinarily nutritious and delicious and easy to prepare. You just soak the seeds overnight in coconut milk and you have the base of your dessert ready to go. If you prefer, you can use almond milk in place of coconut milk. I've also served this pudding topped with homemade jam when blueberries were not in season.

⅓ cup chia seeds

1¾ cups unsweetened coconut milk (one 13.5-ounce can)

3 tablespoons honey or agave nectar

¼ teaspoon cardamom powder

2 pinches of sea salt

1 cup blueberries

1½ teaspoons granulated jaggery or brown sugar

Chopped pistachios or sliced almonds, for garnish

Shredded or chopped dried coconut, for garnish

In a bowl, mix the chia seeds, coconut milk, honey, cardamom powder, and salt together. Refrigerate overnight.

You can choose to serve your chia pudding with warm blueberries or cooled, depending on your preference. If going with the cooled option, you can make the blueberries the day before and chill them in the refrigerator.

Preheat the oven to 425°F. Place the blueberries in a baking dish. Sprinkle the jaggery on top and mix. Roast the blueberries for 14 to 16 minutes, stirring them a few times so they cook evenly. They are done when the berries are exuding their juices but they still hold their shape. There may be one or two that have collapsed, which is fine. Depending on the ripeness of your berries, they may take less time to get to this point, so keep an eye on them. Make sure that a majority of the blueberries are plump, so when you bite into one, you get a burst of juice.

Serve the chia pudding topped with the roasted blueberries, warm or chilled, and a garnish of chopped pistachios and dried coconut on top.

SUMMER PEACHES IN SWEETENED YOGURT *Shrikhand*

(G) Summer • Serves 4

Shrikhand is a dessert made from thick, strained yogurt that is sweetened with powdered sugar and flavored with saffron and cardamom. It is found in Karnataka but has roots in the neighboring state of Maharashtra as well as in Gujarat, farther north.

One version of shrikhand, called aamrakhand, is prepared with mango pulp mixed into the strained yogurt. The yogurt used in this dessert is similar to labneh, a thick Middle Eastern yogurt that is available in some markets. Greek yogurt is not as thick but can be used in a pinch.

In my version, I use juicy peaches, which we get in abundance during the summer, and I garnish it with nuts and seeds. I have also garnished this dessert with fresh blueberries, or if I have more time, I top it with the roasted and cooled jaggery blueberries from my chia pudding recipe (page 159).

4 cups plain whole-milk yogurt*

Pinch of saffron

1 tablespoon warm milk

2 large, ripe peaches

½ teaspoon cardamom powder

About ½ cup powdered sugar

2 tablespoons chopped pistachios or sliced almonds

Pumpkin or chia seeds, for garnish

*Yields will vary, but the goal is to end up with 2 cups of strained yogurt. You can substitute 2⅔ cups of Greek yogurt and strain it slightly, or use 2 cups of labneh, which will not need to be strained further.

Spread out two or three layers of cheesecloth in a mixing bowl. Place the yogurt in the center. Gather the ends of the cheesecloth so that you have a tight ball of yogurt at the bottom. Using a rubber band, fasten the cheesecloth ends together right above the yogurt ball. Lay a wooden spoon across the top of a bowl. Tie the ends of the cheesecloth around the middle of the wooden spoon so that the ball of yogurt is suspended. Leave it in the refrigerator to drain overnight.

Put the saffron in the warm milk. Let stand for 30 minutes.

Peel and pit one of the peaches and puree in a food processor until smooth. You will get about ½ cup of puree, depending on how juicy your peaches are. Chop the second peach into small cubes for garnish.

Transfer the strained yogurt to a large bowl. Mix in the saffron milk, cardamom powder, and powdered sugar. Mix in the peach puree. Taste and add more sugar if your peaches are tart in flavor. Mix in the chopped nuts, reserving a few for garnish.

Serve the yogurt with a garnish of nuts, seeds, and cut peaches. You can chill the dessert further if you'd like a thicker consistency.

APPLE, GINGER, AND COCONUT HAND PIES *Kadabu*

Summer, Fall, Winter • Makes 16 kadabu

Kadabu is a sweet dumpling usually prepared on Ganesha Chaturthi, a Hindu festival honoring the elephant god Ganesh. The dumplings are made with a variety of different flours, including rice, semolina, and all-purpose. Fillings range from simple jaggery (unrefined sugarcane), coconut, and ghee to more involved preparations of cooked and sweetened dals. Kadabu is either steamed or fried.

My recipe for kadabu is strongly influenced by my love for both apple pie and my friend Brigitte Helzer's Alsatian tart dough. I have adapted her recipe to include Indian semolina flour or Cream of Wheat. The kadabu are filled with apples, ginger, coconut, jaggery, saffron, and spices and are baked as opposed to being fried and steamed. You will have more apple filling than you need, but leftovers go wonderfully on ice cream for a quick dessert.

DOUGH

⅔ cup fine Indian semolina or Cream of Wheat

1⅓ cups all-purpose flour

¼ teaspoon salt

¾ cup (1½ sticks) cold unsalted butter, diced

⅓ cup ice water

APPLE FILLING

1½ tablespoons ghee (page 202), unsalted butter, or coconut oil

4 Fuji or Honeycrisp apples, peeled and diced in ½-inch pieces

½ cup granulated jaggery

1½ teaspoons peeled, grated fresh ginger

½ teaspoon cinnamon powder

4 cloves, ground (¼ teaspoon)

Pinch of ground nutmeg

Pinch of saffron

¼ teaspoon salt

½ cup dried unsweetened shredded coconut

1 tablespoon freshly squeezed lemon juice

Cream or whole milk, for brushing

To make the dough: Combine the semolina and all-purpose flours, salt, and butter in a food processor. Add the ice water slowly while pulsing until the dough gets clumpy. Lay a piece of plastic wrap on the counter. Empty the dough onto the plastic wrap and gather it together. Do not overhandle it. Fold the plastic wrap over the dough, and put it in the refrigerator for 30 minutes.

To make the filling: Melt the ghee in a sauté pan over medium heat. Add the apples to the pan. Stir and sauté until just starting to soften, a few minutes. Stir in the jaggery. Add the grated ginger, cinnamon, cloves, nutmeg, saffron, and salt. Continue to cook and stir until the apples start to break down, about 4 minutes. Stir in the coconut and cook for another minute. Stir in the lemon juice and turn off the heat. Transfer the mixture to a plate to cool completely.

Preheat the oven to 375°F. Lightly grease a sheet pan and set aside.

Divide the dough into 16 pieces. On a floured surface, roll out a piece of dough to a circle ⅛ inch thick and 4 inches in diameter. Place 1 tablespoon of filling in the center. Fold the dough in half. Press down at the seam to seal, and use a fork to make indentations all along the seam. Place the pie on the prepared sheet pan. Repeat with the rest of the dough and filling.

Brush each pie with cream. Then score each with a knife. Bake until the pies are golden brown and lightly toasted, 25 to 30 minutes. Serve warm.

CARDAMOM OATMEAL COOKIES WITH DARK CHOCOLATE AND GOLDEN RAISINS

All seasons • Makes about 28 cookies

My oatmeal cookie is spiked with a hint of cardamom, chunks of dark chocolate, and golden raisins. I also use jaggery (unrefined sugarcane) in place of brown sugar for a richer molasses flavor. This recipe is a combination of two cookies from my past: the benne or butter biscuit with cardamom from the famous Iyengar bakeries of Bangalore and a memorable oatmeal cookie from my roommate at Berkeley, talented baker Stephanie Rosemberg.

I usually bake half of the cookies right away and then store the rest of the dough in the freezer for last-minute baking.

½ cup walnuts

2½ cups old-fashioned rolled oats

¾ cup golden raisins

1½ cups (7.5 ounces) dark, bittersweet, or semisweet chocolate chips or chunks

1¼ cups all-purpose flour

1 teaspoon baking soda

½ teaspoon salt

1 teaspoon cardamom powder

½ teaspoon cinnamon powder

1 cup (2 sticks) unsalted butter, at room temperature

¾ cup granulated sugar

¾ cup granulated jaggery or brown sugar

2 eggs

1 teaspoon vanilla extract

Put a small cast-iron frying pan or heavy pan over medium heat. When the pan is warm, add the walnuts and stir until they are golden brown and toasted, 1 or 2 minutes. Set aside on a plate to cool. When cooled, coarsely chop the nuts.

In a medium bowl, mix together the oats, golden raisins, chocolate chips, and chopped walnuts.

In a separate medium bowl, whisk together the flour, baking soda, salt, cardamom, and cinnamon.

Cream the butter, sugar, and jaggery in a mixing bowl. Beat in the eggs and vanilla until combined.

Gradually add the flour mixture to the creamed butter and sugar to combine. Fold in the oats mixture. Make sure to not overmix.

Chill the dough in the refrigerator for 20 minutes. Meanwhile, preheat the oven to 350°F and line a rimmed baking sheet with parchment paper.

Scoop up about 2½ tablespoons of dough and gently roll into a ball. Place on the baking sheet. Repeat to fill the baking sheet, spacing the dough balls 2 inches apart. Wrap any remaining dough in clear plastic wrap in the shape of a log and store in the freezer to bake another time.

Bake until golden brown on top and a smidge darker at the edges, 12 to 14 minutes, rotating the pan 180 degrees halfway through baking. Take the pan out of the oven. The cookies will be delicate, and some may look uncooked in places, but they will harden up as they cool. Cool the cookies on the pan for 5 minutes and then transfer them to a rack to cool further. (If baking additional batches, make sure your baking sheet is completely cool before putting more cookie dough on it.)

You can store the cookies in an airtight container for up to 3 days.

DRIED FRUIT AND NUT DESSERT BALLS *Ladoo*

Ⓥ Ⓖ All seasons • Makes 15 ladoos

Ladoos are Indian dessert balls. There are hundreds of varieties of them, made from different types of flours, nuts, seeds, and dried fruits. I prefer to make my ladoos from Mejdool dates because they are naturally sweet and do not require any additional sugar. They are also very sticky, so the ladoo mixture comes together quite easily. I make this recipe with dried apricots for some tanginess, along with a host of different nuts, cardamom, honey, and coconut.

These ladoos are the perfect sweet ending to a meal, or a healthy pick-me-up during the day. My in-laws love this recipe and take ladoos along on bike rides for a boost of energy.

1 cup raw nuts (almonds, pistachios, cashews)*

2 pinches of fleur de sel or flaky sea salt

⅓ cup dried unsweetened shredded coconut

¾ cup dried Medjool dates

¼ cup dried apricots; you can also use dried figs, cherries, or cranberries

⅛ teaspoon cardamom powder

1 teaspoon ghee (page 202), unsalted butter, or coconut oil

1½ teaspoons honey

*You can make this recipe with preroasted unsalted nuts as well.

Put a cast-iron frying pan or heavy pan over medium heat. When hot, add the nuts. Stir them around until they are roasted and give off a nutty aroma, a few minutes. Transfer to a plate to cool. When cool, coarsely chop the nuts. Mix the nuts with the fleur de sel.

Pulse the coconut in a food processor for 2 or 3 seconds. You don't want to powder it, just make the shreds shorter in length so they are easier to work with. Place the coconut on a plate.

Pulse the dates and apricots in the food processor until they form a pastelike mixture that clumps together. Spread the mixture evenly in the processor and pour the nuts on top, along with the cardamom powder. Pulse until the mixture all comes together. You don't want to powder the nuts, so monitor closely by pulsing for a few seconds at a time and checking the consistency.

Put the ghee in a sauté pan over medium-low heat. When melted, add the date and nut mixture. Mix well to incorporate the ghee evenly. Next, add the honey and mix well. The mixture will start to sizzle; stir and cook it for another minute.

Empty the dried fruit and nut mixture onto a plate. When cooled slightly but still warm to the touch, gather the mixture together with your hands. Take 1 tablespoon of the mixture and roll it into a ball, then roll the ball in the dried coconut. Repeat with the remaining fruit and nut mixture and coconut. (If the coconut is not sticking well, grease your hands with a little ghee or coconut oil. Rub the outside of a ladoo to moisten it, and then roll it in the coconut shreds.)

You can store the ladoos in an airtight container in the refrigerator for up to 1 week.

BANANA, COCONUT, AND CARDAMOM ICE CREAM

Balehannina Rasayana

V G All seasons • Serves 2

Rasayana is a simple but delicious fruit dessert, usually made with cut bananas, jaggery, coconut, and cardamom. I had my first taste of this dessert from my Auntie Latha in Bangalore, but upon coming back to the United States, I found that the bananas here just didn't compare to the varieties found in India.

I then remembered a banana ice cream recipe I had stumbled across a few years back by Faith Durand at The Kitchn website, and I realized that it was my solution! Faith's banana ice cream recipe, one that she developed with her sister, is genius and contains only one ingredient—frozen bananas. They magically turn into fluffy soft serve in your food processor, making the perfect backdrop for jaggery, coconut, and cardamom. And there you have it: rasayana ice cream.

Peel the bananas and cut them into ½-inch disks. Place in a glass bowl or freezer bag. Freeze the bananas for at least 2 hours or up to overnight.

Using a food processor, pulse the frozen banana pieces. They will first get crumbly, then gooey, then look like oatmeal pieces, and then start to bunch on one side of the bowl. Scrape down the sides and keep pulsing through these stages. Eventually, the banana will become smooth and creamy, resembling soft-serve ice cream. Pulse the processor until the mixture aerates and becomes somewhat fluffy, then mix in the coconut, cardamom powder, and chocolate chips.

You can eat the ice cream immediately; it will be like soft-serve ice cream, which is the texture I love, or transfer it to an airtight container and freeze until solid, like traditional ice cream.

Serve with a healthy sprinkling of jaggery, sliced almonds, and more grated coconut on top.

2 ripe bananas

2 tablespoons dried unsweetened shredded coconut, plus more for garnish

¼ teaspoon cardamom powder

1 tablespoon bittersweet or semisweet chocolate chips (optional)

Granulated jaggery or brown sugar, for garnish

Sliced almonds, for garnish

MANGO AND COCONUT MILKSHAKE

Mavina Hannina Seekarne

Ⓖ Summer • Serves 4

In the summer, we buy cases of mangoes from the Indian shops. They are delicious on their own, but for a special treat I make a mango and coconut milkshake based on mavina hannu seekarne. This pudding-like dessert traditionally is made with mango pulp, shredded coconut, milk, and cardamom.

My take on this recipe is a mango and coconut milkshake. In our house, my husband is the smoothie king, so when I told him about this idea of mine, he volunteered his consulting services. This recipe is our collaboration.

2 mangoes, peeled and cubed

1 can (13.5 ounces) unsweetened coconut milk

½ cup plain yogurt

½ teaspoon cardamom powder

3 to 4 tablespoons sugar

2 ice cubes

Place all ingredients in a blender and puree into a shake. Serve immediately.

TURMERIC ALMOND MILK *Badami Haalu*

Ⓖ Winter • Serves 2

The almond milk I grew up drinking is different from the almond milk you buy in grocery stores. It is made from fresh almond paste, whole milk, cardamom, and saffron and is served hot or cold as a sweet treat. I prefer to drink my almond milk warm with a hint of turmeric and garnished with crushed pistachios.

You can omit the turmeric to make the traditional almond milk recipe. In some homes, pistachios or a combination of pistachios and almonds are used in the nut paste.

20 raw almonds

2 cups 2% or whole milk

½ teaspoon turmeric powder

A few saffron threads

¼ teaspoon cardamom powder

About 1 tablespoon sugar

Crushed pistachios, for garnish

Soak the almonds in hot water for 10 to 15 minutes. Peel off the skins of the almonds.

Place the almonds in a blender and grind to a powder. Blend the ground almonds with a couple tablespoons of the milk until you get a fine paste.

Put the rest of the milk in a saucepan over medium heat. When warm, add the almond paste, turmeric powder, saffron, cardamom powder, and sugar. Stir well. Simmer for 4 to 5 minutes, stirring continuously so no skin develops on the top. Taste and add more sugar if necessary.

Serve warm or chilled, garnished with crushed pistachios.

SAVORY SPICED YOGURT DRINK *Majjige* or Buttermilk

G Summer • Serves 2 to 4

I always wondered why, at North Indian restaurants, my mother would order a salty lassi when everyone else was enjoying their sweet mango lassi. I finally understood when I had my first taste of majjige, a delicious savory buttermilk drink from South India.

Traditionally in India, majjige or buttermilk is made from churning homemade yogurt and then removing the butterfat from the top. The resulting buttermilk is flavored with salt, spices, and herbs and served as a digestive at the end of a meal. I make my majjige by blending yogurt and water and flavoring it with cilantro, ginger, black pepper, and spices.

1 cup plain whole-milk yogurt

2 cups water

A few ice cubes

1 teaspoon mild-flavored oil such as canola

¼ teaspoon black mustard seeds

⅛ teaspoon asafetida (hing) powder

½ teaspoon cumin seeds

2 or 3 fresh curry leaves

½ teaspoon freshly ground black pepper, plus more as needed

1½ teaspoons peeled, grated fresh ginger

2 tablespoons cilantro leaves, plus chopped cilantro for garnish

¼ to ½ teaspoon salt

Add the yogurt, water, and ice cubes to a blender. Blend on low speed until combined and frothy on top. You can skim off the froth if you prefer. Transfer the yogurt mixture to another container.

Put the oil in a tempering pot or small pan over medium heat. When the oil is hot and shimmering, add one black mustard seed. When the seed sizzles and pops, add the rest of the mustard seeds and the asafetida. Keep a lid handy to cover the pan while the mustard seeds are popping. When the popping starts to subside (a few seconds), stir in the cumin seeds. When the seeds turn a darker shade of brown (a few seconds), turn the heat to medium-low. Rub the curry leaves between your fingers a little to release their natural oils, and drop them and the black pepper into the oil. Cover immediately, as moisture from the curry leaves will cause the oil to spatter. Then stir to evenly coat everything with oil, a few seconds. Transfer the spices to a bowl to cool.

Once cool, add the spices and curry leaves to the blender with the grated ginger and cilantro. Start grinding, adding just enough of the yogurt mixture to grind the seeds down and get the yogurt to turn a light green color. I usually put my blender on high speed to pulverize the seeds. On low, mix in the rest of the yogurt mixture and ¼ teaspoon of the salt. Taste for salt and black pepper and adjust as needed.

Chill for 30 minutes in the refrigerator to let the flavors marry. If you prefer, you can strain the majjige before serving with a garnish of chopped cilantro leaves.

CHILE WATERMELON JUICE
WITH LIME AND MINT LEAVES

 V G Summer, Fall • Serves 2 to 4

Watermelon season is an exciting time in Bangalore. The green globes flood the markets in bulging piles, and the bright red fruit dominates food carts in bowls and on banana leaves. This juice recipe is inspired by the spicy and sweet watermelon prepared by fruit vendors on the streets of the city.

You'll find the cut fruit served up during the peak of the season with a sprinkle of salt and red chile powder or black pepper. Some vendors sprinkle their fruit with chaat masala, a tangy spice mix originally from North India. You can use black pepper or, if handy, chaat masala instead of the chile powder in this recipe.

Put the water in a small saucepan over medium heat. Stir in the sugar and salt to taste until dissolved. Transfer to another container to cool.

Puree the watermelon chunks in a blender or food processor. Place a bowl underneath a fine-mesh colander. Pour the watermelon pulp into the colander to extract the juice. Push the pulp against the mesh to get as much juice as possible. If you like, save the watermelon pulp for use in a smoothie. Whisk the red chile powder, lime juice, and cooled sugar syrup with the watermelon juice.

Serve over ice with mint leaves and lime wedges.

1 cup water

2 tablespoons sugar

¼ to ½ teaspoon salt

4 cups watermelon chunks, seeded

⅛ teaspoon red chile powder or cayenne pepper, to taste

Juice of 1 lime (about 3 tablespoons)

Ice cubes, for serving

Mint leaves, for serving

Lime wedges, for serving

SOUTH INDIAN DRIP COFFEE *Filter Coffee*

G All seasons • Serves 2 to 4

Coffee is the hot beverage of choice in South India, where coffee plantations abound. I always look forward to my first cup of filter coffee in Bangalore. The filter coffee process is very similar to that of drip coffee but uses a two-chambered stainless steel coffee filter. You can find one at an Indian shop or online, or use a French press.

The coffee is finely ground from arabica or robusta beans with chicory, a plant that enhances its taste. You can purchase an Indian variety like Cothas Coffee or use Café du Monde brand coffee from New Orleans, which includes chicory.

Usually a very small amount of strong coffee is mixed with generous amounts of milk and sugar. In homes, filter coffee is served in 6-ounce stainless steel cups with a curved lip at the top so you can hold them when piping hot.

To make ginger coffee, add 1 teaspoon of peeled, grated fresh ginger to the coffee grounds and an additional 1 teaspoon of sugar to the milk.

For iced filter coffee, allow your coffee to drip overnight and refrigerate once the filter has cooled. In the morning, pour the coffee over ice with cold milk and sugar.

Bring the water to a boil in a kettle or pot.

If using a stainless steel coffee filter, place the ground coffee in a single layer in the top chamber. Gently place the screen with a handle on top of the coffee grounds. Using the handle, turn the screen around to more evenly spread the grounds below. Make sure not to press too hard, as you don't want to pack the coffee too tight, or water will not filter through. First pour a splash of the boiling water on top to allow the coffee grounds to moisten and bloom. Pour the rest of the boiling water on top in a swirling action. Close the lid. Wait until the water has dripped through and a thick coffee decoction has formed on the bottom, 10 to 15 minutes. Check under the screen to make sure the water has completely dripped through. If not, wait a few minutes more. Be careful when opening the filter, as the stainless steel will be very hot.

While the coffee is dripping, heat the milk and sugar in a saucepan. You can add more or less sugar to suit your taste. Stir to dissolve the sugar. Do not let it boil.

Pour equal amounts of the hot milk mixture into coffee cups or stainless steel tumblers. Add the desired amount of coffee and mix well. To get a frothy look, pour the coffee back and forth between two stainless steel tumblers before serving.

You can actually pour more boiling water over the grounds for a second decoction. It will be weaker, but sometimes this is used for an afternoon coffee.

1½ cups water

¼ cup finely ground* dark-roast coffee with chicory

1½ cups 2% or whole milk

About 2 tablespoons sugar

*Similar to an espresso grind.

8

CHUTNEYS AND PICKLES

Condiments play an integral role in an Indian meal. The ingredients used vary from region to region, but the purpose is the same—to elevate the flavor of a dish. Chutneys are probably the most well-known Indian condiment, and in South India the majority of the chutneys my family makes are coconut based with some heat to them (pages 179 to 183). Related to chutneys are spice seasonings that can be sprinkled onto dishes as a finishing touch. The one our family prepares is called chutney pudi (page 190), which translates to "chutney powder." It's so delicious that my family has taken to sprinkling it on many things outside of Indian dishes, including pizza and popcorn.

Hot pickles, referred to as uppinakayi in Kannada and achaar in Hindi, are a more intensely flavored condiment than chutneys. They are called *pickles* because they are made from seasonal produce like green mangoes that have been preserved in a spicy chile brine. You use this condiment sparingly to give meals a spicy, salty, and sour kick. My grandmother had a penchant for pickling, and now so do I. I share her recipe for lemon pickle on page 185.

CILANTRO COCONUT CHUTNEY

G Summer, Fall • Makes 2 cups

This is the chutney I make most often. Coconut chutney (pictured in far left bowl) is the quintessential South Indian condiment. My mother would usually make her coconut chutney with cilantro leaves, as opposed to the more traditional mint leaves. Like her, I am a huge cilantro fan and enjoy any recipe where it has a starring role. It is usually served with idlis (pages 45 to 48), dosas (pages 38 to 44), or fried appetizers but is equally delicious on a sandwich or just mixed with hot rice.

This recipe is essentially two chutney recipes in one, because if you are short on time, you can skip the last step of frying the spices in oil. The majority of the chutneys made in our family use roasted chana dal to give the chutney body and creamy texture, but you can substitute blanched almonds or leave them out for a perfectly tasty chutney. I have also made this recipe with basil leaves or a mixture of mint and cilantro leaves.

Serve with dosa or idli, or as a condiment with any meal. It also goes great on sandwiches, tacos, or eggs and is a perfect accompaniment to appetizers like shishito pepper bhajji (page 148) or lettuce "dosa" wrap (page 145).

¾ cup unsweetened grated coconut (fresh, frozen, or dried)

3 tablespoons roasted chana dal (chana dalia)*

1-inch piece fresh ginger, peeled

2 or 3 Indian green chiles or serrano chiles, stems removed

½ small red onion or 1 shallot, quartered

¼ to ½ cup water, or more as needed

2 cups packed cilantro leaves and thin stems

2 tablespoons freshly squeezed lemon juice, plus more as needed

¼ to ½ teaspoon salt

¼ cup plain yogurt

1 teaspoon mild-flavored oil such as canola

½ teaspoon black mustard seeds

Pinch of asafetida (hing) powder

½ teaspoon urad dal

3 fresh curry leaves

1 dried red chile, broken in half

*If you have chana dal that is not roasted, you can soak it in hot water for 15 minutes. Otherwise, use blanched almonds or almond flour or leave it out.

Thaw frozen coconut or place dried coconut in a little hot water to plump it up.

In a blender, first grind the roasted chana dal to a powder. Then add the ginger, green chiles, onion, and coconut. Grind, adding as little of the water as possible, just enough to get the blades moving. Next add the cilantro, lemon juice, and ¼ teaspoon of the salt. Add a little more of the water. Keep blending and scraping down the sides. The chutney is done when it reaches a creamy, pastelike consistency but still has some texture from the coconut. If you want a thinner consistency,

continued

CILANTRO COCONUT CHUTNEY *continued*

add more water. At a low speed, add the yogurt and more salt if needed. Transfer the chutney to a bowl. (If you are short on time, you can serve the chutney as is.)

Put the oil in a tempering pot or small pan over medium heat. When the oil is hot and shimmering, add one black mustard seed. When the seed sizzles and pops, add the rest of the mustard seeds and the asafetida. Keep a lid handy to cover the pan while the mustard seeds are popping. When the popping starts to subside (a few seconds), immediately add the urad dal. Stir to coat with oil, and turn the heat to medium-low. Continue to stir the dal so it evenly roasts, until it turns a reddish golden brown and smells nutty, less than a minute. Rub the curry leaves between your fingers a little to release their natural oils, and drop them and the dried red chile into the oil. Cover immediately, as moisture from the curry leaves will cause the oil to spatter. Then stir to evenly coat everything with oil, a few seconds. Turn off the heat.

Immediately pour the oil and spices over the chutney. To get all of the oil out of the pan, put a spoonful or two of the chutney into the pan, stir, and spoon it back into the bowl. Taste for salt and lemon juice and adjust as needed.

The chutney is best served fresh but will last a few days in the refrigerator. If you refrigerate the chutney, it will thicken up; just mix in a little water or lemon juice to return it to the right consistency.

MA'S TOMATO CHUTNEY

Ⓥ Ⓖ Summer, Fall • Makes 2 cups

Whenever I make my mother's tomato chutney, I end up "tasting" it a few too many times, because it's totally addictive. It's different from most tomato chutneys you find in the restaurants, which somewhat resemble spicy ketchups. This chutney (pictured in far right bowl, page 178) is sour and savory from sautéed onion and tomatoes, sweet and creamy from coconut, and spicy from ground red chiles. Traditionally eaten with dosas (pages 38 to 44) or idlis (pages 45 to 48), it also makes a fine spread on sandwiches.

For a variation, you can omit the coconut and use a medium or large onion. Onion is sometimes used as a substitute for coconut in recipes because of its natural sweetness.

1 cup unsweetened grated coconut (fresh, frozen, or dried)

3 teaspoons mild-flavored oil such as canola

¾ teaspoon black mustard seeds

2 pinches of asafetida (hing) powder

6 fresh curry leaves

¼ teaspoon fenugreek seeds

4 or 5 dried red chiles, stems removed and broken in half

1 small red onion, chopped

2 large tomatoes, chopped

½ teaspoon salt

3 tablespoons roasted chana dal (chana dalia)*

½ teaspoon tamarind paste, plus more as needed

¼ to ½ cup water, plus more as needed

½ teaspoon urad dal

*If you have chana dal that is not roasted, you can soak it in hot water for 15 minutes. Otherwise, use blanched almonds or almond flour or leave it out.

Thaw frozen coconut or place dried coconut in a little hot water to plump it up.

Heat 2 teaspoons of the oil in a sauté pan over medium heat. When the oil is hot and shimmering, add one black mustard seed. When the seed sizzles and pops, add ½ teaspoon of the mustard seeds and half the asafetida. Keep a lid handy to cover the pan while the mustard seeds are popping. When the popping starts to subside (a few seconds), turn the heat to medium-low. Rub 4 of the curry leaves between your fingers a little to release their natural oils. Drop the leaves, fenugreek seeds, and dried red chiles into the oil. Cover

continued

MA'S TOMATO CHUTNEY *continued*

immediately, as moisture from the curry leaves will cause the oil to spatter. Then stir to evenly coat everything with oil, and cook until the fenugreek seeds turn a darker golden color and smell fragrant, a few seconds longer. The seeds will become bitter if fried for too long, so keep an eye on them.

Add the onion to the pan and sauté over medium heat until softened, another minute. Next, stir in the tomatoes and ¼ teaspoon of the salt and cook, covered, until the tomatoes are softened and cooked through, 7 to 8 minutes. Turn off the heat. Transfer the mixture to a plate to cool.

In a blender, first grind the roasted chana dal to a powder. Then add the cooked tomato mixture and puree. Next add the coconut, tamarind paste, and just enough of the water to get the blades moving. Keep blending and scraping down the sides. The chutney is done when it reaches a creamy, paste-like consistency but still has some texture from the coconut. If you want a thinner consistency, add more water. Transfer the chutney to a bowl. (If you are short on time, you can serve the chutney as is, tasting for salt and adjusting as needed.)

Put the remaining 1 teaspoon oil in the sauté pan over medium heat. When the oil is hot and shimmering, add one black mustard seed. When the seed sizzles and pops, add the remaining ¼ teaspoon of black mustard seeds and the remaining asafetida. Keep a lid handy to cover the pan while the mustard seeds are popping. When the popping starts to subside (a few seconds), immediately add the urad dal. Stir to coat with oil, and turn the heat to medium-low. Continue to stir the dal so it roasts evenly, until it turns a reddish golden brown and smells nutty, less than a minute. Rub the remaining curry leaves between your fingers a little to release their natural oils, and drop them into the oil. Cover immediately, as moisture from the curry leaves will cause the oil to spatter. Then stir to evenly coat everything with oil, a few seconds. Turn off the heat.

Immediately pour the oil and spices over the chutney. To get all of the oil out of the pan, put a spoonful or two of the chutney into the pan, stir, and spoon it back into the bowl. Taste for salt and tamarind and adjust as needed.

The chutney is best served fresh but will last a few days in the refrigerator. If you refrigerate the chutney, it will thicken up; just mix in a little water to return it to the right consistency.

CARAMELIZED SHALLOT, ALMOND, AND RED CHILE CHUTNEY

 All seasons • Makes about ¾ cup

When my mother was away on business trips, my father would make some of his signature dishes, one of which was cumin rice mixed with caramelized onions. At the time, if you had asked my father or me what a caramelized onion was, we probably both would have shrugged; my father just instinctively cooked his onions until they turned brown in color and so sweet in flavor.

My shallot chutney recipe is inspired by those onions and a red chile chutney that is often served with dosa in South India. After cooking the shallots on low heat for about an hour with dried red chiles, I reduce them in a sauce of tamarind and jaggery and then blend them into a creamy chutney with blanched almonds. The flavors are sweet, spicy, and sour and pair perfectly with a dosa (pages 38 to 44), an idli (pages 45 to 48), rice, or a cheese sandwich.

2 tablespoons mild-flavored oil such as canola

½ teaspoon black mustard seeds

1 teaspoon urad dal

3 or 4 fresh curry leaves

4 or 5 dried red chiles, stems removed, broken in half

3 or 4 shallots (about 8 ounces), peeled and coarsely chopped

¼ teaspoon salt

About 1 teaspoon tamarind paste

1½ teaspoons granulated jaggery or brown sugar

¾ to 1 cup water, plus more as needed

¼ cup blanched almonds, whole or sliced*

*You can also substitute almond flour.

Put the oil in a frying pan over medium heat. When the oil is hot and shimmering, add one black mustard seed. When the seed sizzles and pops, add the rest of the mustard seeds. Keep a lid handy to cover the pan while the mustard seeds are popping. When the popping starts to subside (a few seconds), immediately add the urad dal. Stir to coat with oil, and turn the heat to medium-low. Continue to stir the dal so it roasts evenly, until it turns a reddish golden brown and smells nutty, less than a minute. Rub the curry leaves between your fingers a little to release their natural oils, and drop them and the dried red chiles into the oil. Cover immediately, as moisture from the curry leaves will cause the oil to spatter. Then stir to evenly coat everything with oil, a few seconds.

Add the shallots to the oil and turn the heat to medium. Stir-fry until softened and translucent, a couple of minutes. Sprinkle with the salt. Turn the heat to medium-low and continue to cook the shallots until they turn brown, about half an hour. Stir them from time to time to keep them from burning. However, it's important to leave the shallots alone enough that they caramelize. They are done when they are nice and browned. When the shallots have caramelized, mix in the tamarind paste, jaggery, and ¼ cup of the water. Bring to a boil and simmer until the liquid evaporates and the mixture thickens, a couple of minutes. Taste for salt and tamarind and adjust as needed. Transfer the shallot mixture to a bowl to cool.

continued

CARAMELIZED SHALLOT, ALMOND, AND RED CHILE CHUTNEY *continued*

In a blender, first grind the blanched almonds to a powder. Then add the cooled shallot mixture and puree. Add just enough of the remaining water to get the blades moving. Keep blending and scraping down the sides. The chutney is done when it reaches a creamy, pastelike consistency. If you want a thinner consistency, add more water. Transfer the chutney to a bowl.

The chutney is best served fresh, but it will last a few days in the refrigerator.

MEYER LEMON PICKLE *Nimbehannu Uppinakayi*

  Winter, Spring • Makes about 2 cups

Pickle, or uppinakayi in Kannada and achaar in Hindi, is a spicy, salty, and sour condiment made from seasonal produce preserved in a chile brine and used sparingly at almost every meal. You can mix into rice, lentils, curries, and yogurt. My grandmother excelled in the art of pickle making and would often have large quantities of pickle fermenting in porcelain crocks, or jaadis. My Meyer lemon pickle is loosely based on her recipes, which were transcribed for me by my Auntie Karen.

Meyer lemons are a cross between a lemon and a mandarin orange and, similar to the lemons and limes found in India, their thin skin is easily softened by salt, which is important here. They are also sweeter and smaller than other varities. I discovered them when I lived in California, where they are abundant during the winter months. For a variation, you can use limes.

6 juicy Meyer lemons, preferably organic*

¼ cup kosher salt (not iodized)

1 teaspoon turmeric powder

1 teaspoon roasted fenugreek powder (page 199)

1 or 2 tablespoons red chile powder or cayenne pepper**

2 tablespoons sunflower or canola oil

1 teaspoon black mustard seeds

¼ teaspoon asafetida (hing) powder

*If your lemons are not that juicy, add the juice from 1 or 2 additional lemons.

**Red chile powder tends to mellow over time, so the pickle will be most spicy when you first make it.

Soak the lemons in water for 5 minutes and then scrub them with a brush to remove any dirt. Dry them with a clean towel. Before working with the lemons, there should not be even a drop of water on them; leaving them out to dry is a good way to ensure this.

On a dry cutting board with a dry knife, remove the tips of the lemons if they are jutting out. Quarter the lemons and remove all of the seeds. Then cut each quarter in half lengthwise. Cut each of these pieces into 3 or 4 bite-size wedges. You should be left with 24 to 32 wedges per lemon. Place all of the lemons and their juices in a large, clean bowl. (If you are using additional lemon juice, add it to the bowl at this time.)

Sterilize a 32-ounce wide-mouthed glass jar with a noncorrosive lid, or use a clean ceramic crock. If you are using a glass jar, you can also place clear plastic wrap on the mouth of the jar before closing the lid. Make sure the jar or crock is completely dry before using. Put a thin layer of salt on the bottom of the glass jar. Sprinkle a little of the turmeric powder over the salt layer. Place a layer of lemon wedges on top of the salt and turmeric. Continue to layer like this until you have used all of the salt, turmeric, and lemon. Make sure to use all of the juice from the lemons and to end with a layer of salt and turmeric.

Cover tightly and let the jar sit in a sunny window for the next 2 weeks, until the lemon skins become soft. Each day, shake or gently stir the lemon

continued

MEYER LEMON PICKLE *continued*

mixture with a clean spoon. As the days go by, more juice will seep out of the lemons, and they will start to shrink in size. When your lemons are ready for the next step, the skins will be soft enough to bite into easily. If they are not there yet, keep going with the daily stirring regimen.

When the lemon skins have softened, empty the contents of the jar into a clean bowl. With a clean, dry spoon, mix the lemon pieces with the fenugreek powder and red chile powder.

Put the oil in a tempering pot or small pan, over medium heat. When the oil is hot and shimmering, add one black mustard seed. When the seed sizzles and pops, add the rest of the mustard seeds and the asafetida. Keep a lid handy to cover the pan while the mustard seeds are popping. When the popping starts to subside (a few seconds), pour the oil and spices into an empty bowl to cool down. Make sure you get all of the oil and spices out of the tempering pot. Hot oil can cause steam and moisture to be created when added to the lemons, which shortens the pickle's shelf life.

When cooled, pour the oil over the lemon pieces. Mix well so all pieces are evenly coated. Return the lemon pickle to its jar. Seal it well and let it sit for a few days or up to a week so that the flavors meld together. After the melding period, you can eat the pickle and store it in the refrigerator. It will keep for several months. When serving, always use a clean spoon and no double-dipping, as this will spoil the pickle.

RHUBARB STRAWBERRY PICKLE

V G Summer • Makes about 1½ cups

Most people love rhubarb for its use in sweet preparations, but I believe in its savory side so much that I make a limited-edition rhubarb ginger achaar at Brooklyn Delhi. In the summer, I get an abundance of rhubarb from our farm share, and it struck me one day that the sourness of rhubarb would make a perfect Indian pickle.

Rhubarb is often paired with strawberries in pies and crumbles for their complementary flavors. I combine the two in this quick pickle with spicy green chiles, ginger, and lemon juice. The result is a sweet and spicy pickle that definitely wakes the senses. You can serve this pickle in a variety of ways: with rice and dal, mixed into a yogurt, or in a spicy mayo for spreading on sandwiches.

1 pound rhubarb

3 tablespoons sunflower or canola oil

½ teaspoon black mustard seeds

⅛ teaspoon asafetida (hing) powder

¼ teaspoon turmeric powder

1 tablespoon peeled, grated fresh ginger

1 Indian green chile or serrano chile, chopped

1 to 2 tablespoons red chile powder or cayenne pepper

½ teaspoon roasted fenugreek powder (page 199)

5 strawberries, sliced

1 tablespoon granulated jaggery or brown sugar

1 tablespoon freshly squeezed lemon juice

½ teaspoon kosher salt (not iodized)

Wash the rhubarb stalks and dry them completely. Trim off the ends. Cut the rhubarb into ½-inch pieces.

Put the oil in a sauté pan over medium heat. When the oil is hot and shimmering, add one black mustard seed. When the seed sizzles and pops, add the rest of the mustard seeds and the asafetida. Keep a lid handy to cover the pan while the mustard seeds are popping. When the popping starts to subside (a few seconds), turn the heat to medium-low. Add the turmeric powder, ginger, and green chiles. Then stir to evenly coat everything with oil and fry until the ginger and chile are less raw, 10 to 15 seconds.

Stir the rhubarb and red chile and fenugreek powders into the pan. Sauté over medium heat until the rhubarb is soft but still holds its shape, 4 or 5 minutes. Add the strawberries, jaggery, lemon juice, and salt. Stir well and cook until the mixture starts looking more saucy from the strawberries cooking down and their juices mingling in the pan, a few minutes more. Turn off the heat.

When the pickle is completely cool, store in a clean, dry jar in the refrigerator. This pickle will keep for 1 to 2 weeks. When serving, always use a clean spoon and no double-dipping, as this will spoil the pickle.

SPICY CRANBERRY RELISH *Thokku*

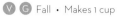 Ⓥ Ⓖ Fall • Makes 1 cup

Thokku is a condiment halfway between a pickle and a chutney. It is usually made from a sour or tart fruit like green mangoes or green gooseberries that are grated and cooked on the stove top with oil, chiles, and spices. My Aunties Asha and Karen both make their thokku from cranberries, which are more easily found at the farmers' market in fall. I've adapted this version from their recipes. I like to add jaggery, an unrefined cane sugar, to balance out the tang of the cranberries and the spiciness of the chiles.

Cranberry thokku has a thick texture, perfect for spreading on sandwiches or mixing into rice, lentils, saaru, or huli (pages 131 to 134). It can also serve as a spicy alternative to sweet cranberry sauce on Thanksgiving.

2 cups cranberries

4 Indian green chiles or serrano chiles, stems removed

⅛ teaspoon plus 1 pinch asafetida (hing) powder

¼ cup sunflower or canola oil, plus more as needed

½ teaspoon black mustard seeds

¼ teaspoon turmeric powder

2 teaspoons kosher salt (not iodized)

1 teaspoon red chile powder or cayenne pepper

½ teaspoon roasted fenugreek powder (page 199)

2 teaspoons granulated jaggery or brown sugar

Wash and pick through the cranberries, discarding any soft ones. Dry the cranberries in a colander. Once they are dry, crush them in a food processor. Set aside. Add the green chiles to the food processor and chop them with the pinch of the asafetida.

Put the oil in a sauté pan over medium heat. When the oil is hot and shimmering, add one black mustard seed. When the seed sizzles and pops, add the rest of the mustard seeds and the ⅛ teaspoon asafetida. Keep a lid handy to cover the pan while the mustard seeds are popping. When the popping starts to subside (a few seconds), turn the heat to medium-low. Add the turmeric powder and chopped green chiles. Then stir to evenly coat everything with oil and fry until the chiles are less raw, 10 to 15 seconds.

Add the crushed cranberries to the pan and mix well. Add the salt, red chile powder, and fenugreek powder. Stir well so the cranberries do not stick to the pan. Add a little more oil if it is looking dry. Continue to cook the cranberries until the mixture forms a ball and comes away from the sides of the pan and the oil separates. The relish should be almost the consistency of peanut butter. This should take about 5 minutes or so. Stir in the jaggery well. Cook for another minute. Turn off the heat.

When the cranberry thokku cools completely, place it in a clean glass jar and store in the refrigerator. It will keep for about a month. When serving, always use a clean spoon and no double-dipping, as this will spoil the thokku.

CHUTNEY POWDER *Chutney Pudi*

 V G All seasons • Makes about 3 cups

There are numerous chutney powders used to accent dishes in South India. The powder condiments are sprinkled on a variety of finished dishes to add a punch of flavor, similar in vein to a North Indian chaat masala, Middle Eastern za'atar or North African dukkah.

My mother would make large quantities of one powder we simply referred to as chutney pudi (pictured in top bowl, page 178), or chutney powder. In some circles, this powder is also lovingly referred to as gunpowder. My mother makes hers from roasted lentils, red chiles, curry leaves, and shredded coconut dried on the roof of our house in Bangalore.

The following powder is adapted from my mother's recipe. Sprinkle it on dosas, mix it with hot rice and butter, or, my personal favorite, scatter it on buttered toast, pizza, or plain yogurt.

1 cup chana dal

½ cup urad dal

4 sprigs curry leaves (about 80 leaves)

1 to 2 tablespoons seedless dried tamarind, diced, or tamarind powder (optional)

2 teaspoons mild-flavored oil such as canola

⅛ teaspoon asafetida (hing) powder

10 to 15 dried red chiles or 18 dried Byadgi chiles, stems removed*

1 cup dried unsweetened shredded coconut

1 teaspoon kosher salt (not iodized)

*I prefer using Byadgi chiles (photo page 197), which are available at Indian shops and online, because they have a subtle spiciness and their deep red color provides a nice hue to the powder. You can also use a combination of dried red and Byadgi chiles. It's best to err on the side of less chile because you can always roast and grind more to add to your powder if you want more heat.

VIBRANT INDIA

190

Put a cast-iron frying pan or other heavy pan over medium-low heat. When hot, add the chana dal and dry-roast, stirring it all the while, until it turns a reddish golden brown and has a nutty aroma. Transfer to a plate to cool. Next add the urad dal to the pan. Dry-roast the urad dal, stirring it all the while, until it turns a reddish golden brown and has a nutty aroma. Transfer to the plate with the roasted chana dal to cool. Add the curry leaves to the pan and roast the leaves, stirring them the entire time, until they have dried and start to curl up. Transfer the leaves to the plate with the roasted dals to cool. Add the diced tamarind to the pan and dry-roast it for a minute, stirring the entire time. Transfer the tamarind to the plate to cool.

Add the oil to the pan. Add the asafetida and fry until you smell an onion-like aroma, a few seconds. Next mix in the dried red chiles, stirring them constantly. When they are fragrant and your nose starts to tingle, add the dried coconut, stirring all the while. You just want to warm the coconut. Turn off the heat and add all of the dry-roasted ingredients to the pan. Add the salt and mix it all well. Let the mixture cool.

Coarsely grind the ingredients in batches in a spice or coffee grinder or in a Vitamix dry ingredient jar. Taste for salt and red chile and adjust if needed. The consistency should not be a fine powder, but should be fine enough to be sprinkled on dishes. Store in an airtight container or jar at room temperature for about a month; it will last for several months if stored in the refrigerator.

9

FROM SCRATCH

You can find most of the items in this chapter at Indian shops or online, but I think sometimes it's fun to make them from scratch.

The two most frequently used spice blends in South India are huli (sambar) powder (page 196) and saaru (rasam) powder (page 194). I have also included one other powder that is a bit more esoteric called vangi baath powder (page 198) that I use quite a bit in my kitchen. These powders are generally made differently throughout regions of South India, but even within my family there are slight variations from household to household. The powders are great to have in bulk as they have a long shelf life and flavor a host of different recipes from the book. I use a Vitamix to grind large batches of spice blends and a coffee grinder that I have designated just for spices for smaller quantities.

For making these spice blends, I highly recommend using a combination of dried red chiles and Byadgi chiles or just Byadgi chiles (photo page 197), a variety grown in Karnataka. Byadgi chiles are wrinkly in appearance, have a mellow heat, and give powders a bright red coloring. They are available at Indian shops and online.

In addition to spice powders, I share my parents' recipes for homemade yogurt and ghee, Indian-style clarified butter.

SAARU (OR RASAM) POWDER *Saarina Pudi*

 All seasons • Makes about 2 cups

Saaru powder is used almost every day in South Indian homes to make a tangy lentil soup called saaru or rasam (pages 125 and 128), depending on what region you are in. The tang usually comes from tamarind, tomatoes, or lemon. My grandmother would send the roasted spices to a local flour mill in Bangalore to be ground fine. This recipe is adapted from my Aunties Shantha and Asha. I like to use this spice mix in a variety of ways besides making saaru, sometimes adding it into stir-fries (pages 80 to 82) or coconut milk curry (page 128).

1 cup coriander seeds

2 tablespoons cumin seeds

2 tablespoons black mustard seeds

1½ tablespoons fenugreek seeds

1 teaspoon ghee (page 202) or canola oil

2 tablespoons whole black peppercorns

2 (3-inch) cinnamon sticks

¾ cup fresh curry leaves, loosely packed (optional)*

40 dried red chiles or 60 dried Byadgi chiles, stems removed*

¼ teaspoon asafetida (hing) powder

1 teaspoon turmeric powder

---

*You can use dried curry leaves or omit them, and instead add them when making the saaru, to give this powder a longer shelf life.

**I prefer using Byadgi chiles (photo page 197), which are available at Indian shops and online, because they have a subtle spiciness and their deep red color provides a nice hue to the powder. You can also use a combination of dried red and Byadgi chiles. It's best to err on the side of less chile because you can always roast and grind more to add to your powder if you want more heat.

In a cast-iron frying pan or other heavy pan over medium-low heat, roast the coriander seeds, stirring them continuously until fragrant. Be watchful that they do not burn. Transfer to a plate to cool. Add the cumin seeds to the pan. Stir and roast until you smell their aroma and the seeds turn golden brown. Transfer them to the plate to cool. Add the black mustard seeds. Stir and fry them until you see a number of them popping in the pan. Transfer to the plate to cool. Add the fenugreek seeds to the pan. Stir and roast them until they turn golden brown and have a nutty aroma. Transfer to the plate to cool.

Add ½ teaspoon of the ghee to the pan. When melted, add the black peppercorns and cinnamon sticks and stir and fry until they are fragrant and sputter. Transfer to the plate to cool. Add another ¼ teaspoon ghee to the pan. When melted, add the curry leaves, if using. Roast the leaves, stirring, until they have dried and start to curl up. Transfer the leaves to the plate to cool.

Add the remaining ¼ teaspoon of ghee to the pan. When melted, add the dried red chiles. Stir and fry them until they warm up and become fragrant, and your nose starts to tickle. Turn off the heat. Add the rest of the roasted ingredients to the pan and mix.

Cool the spices and grind them to a fine powder in a spice grinder or powerful blender. Mix in the asafetida and turmeric powder. Store in an airtight container for several months at room temperature, and longer in the refrigerator.

HULI (OR SAMBAR) POWDER *Huli Pudi*

Ⓥ Ⓖ All seasons • Makes about 3 cups

Huli powder is used almost every day in the house to make a lentil and vegetable stew called huli or sambar (pages 131 to 137). I also use it to flavor some of my vegetable stir-fry and rice dishes and green beans. What's interesting is that this "spice blend" is actually made from a good portion of roasted lentils, which makes it rich in protein just by itself. This recipe is adapted from my mother's maternal Aunt Sundru, by way of my Auntie Asha.

¾ cup chana dal

½ teaspoon urad dal

About 1½ teaspoons mild-flavored oil such as canola

2 cups coriander seeds

60 dried red chiles or 90 dried Byadgi chiles, stems removed*

4 (3-inch) cinnamon sticks

1½ teaspoons fenugreek seeds

1 cup fresh curry leaves, loosely packed (optional)**

½ cup dried unsweetened shredded coconut (optional)**

1½ teaspoons turmeric powder

---

*I prefer using Byadgi chiles (photo, right), which are available at Indian shops and online, because they have a subtle spiciness and their deep red color provides a nice hue to the powder. You can also use a combination of dried red and Byadgi chiles. It's best to err on the side of less chile because you can always roast and grind more to add to your powder if you want more heat.

**You can omit the curry leaves and coconut, and instead add them when making the huli, to give this powder a longer shelf life.

Put a cast-iron frying pan or other heavy pan over medium-low heat. When hot, add the chana dal and dry-roast, stirring it all the while, until it turns a reddish golden brown and has a nutty aroma. This may take several minutes, so be patient. Transfer to a plate to cool. Next add the urad dal to the pan. Dry-roast the urad dal, stirring it all the while, until it turns a reddish golden brown and has a nutty aroma. Transfer to the plate with the chana dal to cool.

The next group of spices each needs to be fried separately in a bit of oil. It takes patience, but this step is important because each spice takes a different amount of time to roast. Add ½ teaspoon of the oil to the pan. Add the coriander seeds. Roast and stir continuously until they are fragrant. Be watchful that the seeds do not burn. Transfer to a plate to cool.

Add another ¼ teaspoon oil to the pan. Add the dried red chiles. Stir and fry them until they warm up and become fragrant and your nose starts to tickle. Transfer to the plate to cool.

Add ⅛ teaspoon of the oil to the pan and add the cinnamon sticks. Stir and fry until fragrant. Transfer to the plate to cool.

Add ⅛ teaspoon of the oil to the pan and add the fenugreek seeds. Stir and fry until they turn golden brown and have a nutty aroma. Transfer to the plate to cool.

Add the remaining ⅛ teaspoon of oil to the pan and add the curry leaves, if using. Roast the leaves, stirring them the entire time, until they have dried and start to curl up. Transfer to the plate to cool.

Add the coconut, if using, to the pan. Stir it until it just warms up and becomes fragrant. Transfer it to the plate to cool.

Grind the cooled spices, curry leaves, and coconut to a powder in a spice grinder or powerful blender. This powder is not as fine as rasam powder and will be somewhat coarse. Mix in the turmeric powder.

Store in an airtight container or glass jar. It will keep for several months at room temperature, and longer if stored in the refrigerator.

VANGI BAATH POWDER *Vangi Baath Pudi*

V G All seasons • Makes about 2 cups

Vangi baath powder is the spice blend used to make vangi baath, an eggplant rice dish (page 106), but it's also great to have around to spice up rice and vegetable stir-fries or roasted vegetables (page 85). This recipe was passed down from my Aunties Karen and Latha, who learned it from my grandmother.

½ cup chana dal

¼ cup urad dal

¾ cup coriander seeds

About ½ teaspoon mild-flavored oil such as canola

25 dried red chiles or 35 dried Byadgi chiles, stems removed*

1-inch cinnamon stick

3 cloves

---

*I prefer using Byadgi chiles (photo page 197), which are available at Indian shops and online, because they have a subtle spiciness and their deep red color provides a nice hue to the powder. You can also use a combination of dried red and Byadgi chiles. It's best to err on the side of less chile because you can always roast and grind more to add to your powder if you want more heat.

Put a cast-iron frying pan or other heavy pan over medium-low heat. When hot, add the chana dal and dry-roast, stirring it all the while, until it turns a reddish golden brown and has a nutty aroma. This may take several minutes, so be patient. Transfer to a plate to cool. Next add the urad dal to the pan. Dry-roast the urad dal, stirring it all the while, until it turns a reddish golden brown and has a nutty aroma. Transfer to the plate with the chana dal to cool.

Add the coriander seeds to the pan. Roast and continuously stir until fragrant. Be watchful that the seeds do not burn. Transfer to the plate to cool.

Add ⅛ teaspoon of the oil to the pan. Add the dried red chiles. Stir and fry them until they warm up and become fragrant and your nose starts to tickle. Transfer to the plate to cool.

Add ⅛ teaspoon of the oil to the pan and add the cinnamon stick. Stir and fry until fragrant. Transfer to the plate to cool.

Add ⅛ teaspoon of the oil to the pan and add the cloves. Stir and fry until fragrant. Transfer to the plate to cool.

Grind the cooled dal spices to a fine powder in a spice grinder or powerful blender.

Store in an airtight container or glass jar. It will keep for several months at room temperature, and longer if stored in the refrigerator.

ROASTED FENUGREEK SEED POWDER *Menthyada Pudi*

V G All seasons • Makes about ½ cup

Roasted fenugreek seed powder is rarely found in Indian shops, so I wanted to include a bulk recipe for it, as I like to have it on hand for sprinkling into stir-fries (pages 80 to 82) or coconut curries called gojju (pages 88 to 90), making pickles (pages 185 to 189), or adding to dosa batters (pages 38 to 44).

The powder adds a nutty, almost maple flavor to dishes. You must be very mindful when you are roasting fenugreek seeds because they will burn and become bitter in the blink of an eye. I like to roast them until they are just golden brown and have a nutty aroma.

7 tablespoons fenugreek seeds

In a cast-iron frying pan or other heavy pan, over medium-low heat, roast the fenugreek seeds, stirring all the while, until they turn golden brown and have a nutty aroma. Immediately transfer them to a plate to cool. Grind to a fine powder in a spice grinder or powerful blender. Store in an airtight container or jar.

YOGURT *Mosaru*

Yogurt, known as mosaru in Kannada, can also be made in the home. I grew up eating homemade yogurt and learned to make it by watching my mother and father. Yogurt is a lot like bread, in that you have to make it a few times to really get it right, because different factors such as climate will affect how well it sets. I have to admit, though, that the experimentation is worth it because there's nothing more satisfying than eating homemade yogurt.

4 cups milk, preferably whole

2 tablespoons plain yogurt*

---

*Yogurt from a previous yogurt batch has live bacteria culture and is the key ingredient for fermentation. You can also substitute yogurt starter, found at most health food stores or even just store-bought yogurt.

Bring the milk to a boil in a saucepan (I use a CorningWare square casserole dish because that is what my mother always used) over medium-high heat. Stir the milk from time to time while it heats up, so it does not scorch on the bottom. If using a thermometer, make sure the milk gets to at least 180°F. Heating the milk kills any competing bacteria and also changes the protein in the milk to allow it to ferment. A layer of cream often forms on top of the boiling milk. You can take the layer off, but I prefer to keep it. This cream part is referred to as *kennai* in Kannada.

Once the milk has boiled, simmer it for about 5 minutes and stir with a spoon. This step is optional, but it is a practice that my mother passed on to me.

If you are using a saucepan to heat your milk, you may want to transfer the milk to a bowl or dish that you can easily store in your refrigerator. Cool the milk until it is lukewarm to the touch, 110° to 115°F on a thermometer. It will take about half an hour to cool.

In a small bowl, combine ¼ cup of the warm milk and 1 tablespoon of the yogurt. Whisk them together gently so the yogurt is fully incorporated. Mix the dissolved yogurt into the rest of the milk.

Take the remaining 1 tablespoon of yogurt and rub it along the inside walls of the yogurt pot. This is a tip my father passed on to me. He told me the walls of the dish are actually where the fermentation of the yogurt begins.

Cover the dish and place it in the oven with the light on. If you don't have an oven light, wrap your yogurt pot in blankets or a towel to keep it warm. The correct temperature for setting yogurt is 110° to 115°F. The yogurt should set within 5 to 10 hours. I usually just leave it in the oven overnight.

Store the yogurt in the refrigerator, and use it within 2 weeks. (Set aside 2 tablespoons of the set yogurt for making your next batch.)

INDIAN-STYLE CLARIFIED BUTTER *Ghee or Thuppa*

Ⓖ All seasons • Makes about ¾ cup

Ghee, or thuppa in Kannada, is traditionally made with the cream from homemade yogurt in India. The cream is churned to make butter and then cooked to make ghee. The method for making ghee is the same as the one for clarifying butter, but for ghee you cook the butter longer to result in caramelized and browned milk solids and pure butterfat, resembling the hue of golden honey with a nutty aroma and flavor. The best-tasting ghee is made from cultured butter, but good-quality unsalted butter will also do the trick.

In Hinduism, ghee is viewed as holy and is a key ingredient in many sweets prepared for religious festivals. For centuries, ghee has been used in ayurvedic medicine to treat constipation and ulcers. Since you boil away the milk solids in butter to make ghee, it does not need to be refrigerated.

1 cup (2 sticks) unsalted butter, cut into 1-inch pieces

Melt the butter in a saucepan over medium-low heat. You'll hear a crackling, which means the butter is boiling. At this point, there will be bubbles and a layer of foam forming on the top, yellow clarifying butter in the middle, and milk solids at the bottom. Using a spoon, skim the foam off the top.

Turn the heat to low so that you can still hear the crackling and slow bubbling. Keep skimming the foam off the top. The butter's color will change from yellow to golden. Make sure to stir from time to time so the milk solids don't burn. When the crackling subsides, the butter will be a clear golden color and the milk solids below will be a light brown. The time it takes to get to this point will differ, depending on how much water is in the butter.

Turn off the heat and take the pan off the stove. When the ghee is cool, strain it into a glass jar using a fine-mesh strainer (I use two tea strainers) or three layers of cheesecloth. Make sure there are no solids in the ghee jar. One trick is to let the ghee solidify and then just scoop out the ghee on top, leaving the bottom layer, as that is where the milk solids settle. (You can use the milk solids and any other residuals from making ghee by mixing them into rice or spreading them on toast.)

Ghee will last for up to 2 months at room temperature, longer if stored in the refrigerator.

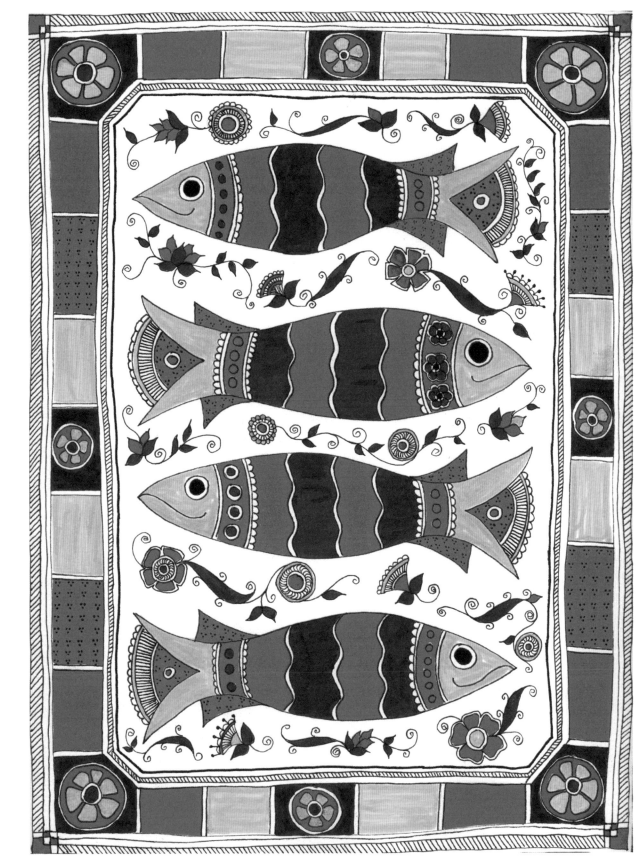

HANDS OVER FORKS
AND KNIVES

I have always eaten food with my hand, and that's not just pizza and tacos or naan and curry. I mean rice with soupy dals and the like. This is normal practice all over India, and I never thought twice about it until I moved out of my parents' house. Once I was living on my own, I refrained from doing so in front of friends, but I've come back to it now, even showing people how to do it and incorporating the practice into my cooking classes.

There is something that happens to the flavor of food when mixed with your hand that cannot be duplicated with a fork and knife. Especially since a South Indian meal is so modular, eating with your hands helps you to combine flavors on your plate in the most optimal way. During my visits to my mother's childhood home in Bangalore, I looked forward to having my grandmother mix my food with her hands, because somehow it always tasted better than if I did it myself.

To eat with your hand, use one hand only, your dominant hand—traditionally it was taboo to eat with your left hand but times have changed. If you are eating rice, huli (lentil stew), and a hot pickle, for instance, you would mix it all up well with one hand and then pick up a bite-size portion with your fingers and push it into your mouth using your thumb. Everyone has their own style, but that is mine. Some pros will form balls quickly with their hand and literally throw them in their mouth, never missing a beat.

I hope you give eating with your hand a try. It takes a little practice, but it will transform the way you taste Indian food.

MEAL PLANNING AND SAMPLE MENUS

Indian meals are modular, with a number of different dishes served together. For instance, a vegetable stir-fry in the book may serve four, but it functions more as a side dish than a main course.

I tend to favor bowl dinners on weekdays and may make rice and a lentil dish. I have a side of plain yogurt at every meal, and at most I have a hot pickle or one of my achaars from Brooklyn Delhi on the side. On days when I have more time, I will also prepare a vegetable stir-fry, a salad, or a yogurt raita. On the weekend, I may make a flavored rice dish from leftover rice in the fridge.

YOUR FIRST SOUTH INDIAN MEAL

Lemon Peanut Rice (*Nimbehannu Chitranna*), page 103

Potato, Carrot, and Red Lentil Stew (*Tharakaari Huli* or *Sambar*), page 131

Radish Yogurt Raita, page 74

Chia Pudding with Roasted Jaggery Blueberries (*Sabbakki Payasa*), page 159

SPRING MEAL

Spiced Spring Vegetable and Coconut Polenta (*Uppittu* or *Upma*), page 55

Rhubarb Strawberry Pickle, page 188, or Brooklyn Delhi Rhubarb Ginger Achaar

Banana, Coconut and Cardamom Ice Cream (*Nimbehannu Sabseege Soppina Baath*), page 167

SUMMER MEAL

Lime Dill Rice with Pistachios (*Nimbehannu Sabseege Soppina Baath*), page 104

Summer Squash in Herby Coconut Yogurt Curry (*Majjige Huli*), page 69

Summer Peaches in Sweetened Yogurt (*Shrikhand*), page 160

FALL MEAL

Spicy and Sour Tomato Lentil Soup (*Tomato Bele Saaru* or *Rasam*), page 125

Green Bean and Coconut Stir-Fry (*Huralikayi Palya*), page 82

Turmeric Rice, page 100 or 101

Apple, Ginger, and Coconut Hand Pies (*Kadabu*), page 163

WINTER MEAL

Brown Rice

Roasted Kabocha Squash and Coconut Milk Soup, page 128

Kale Yogurt Raita, page 75

Cardamom Oatmeal Cookies with Dark Chocolate and Golden Raisins, page 164

WHERE TO BUY INGREDIENTS AND EQUIPMENT

Nowadays, there are several resources for finding an Indian shop near you or for ordering ingredients online.

DIRECTORY OF INDIAN GROCERS IN THE UNITED STATES

If you live in the United States, you can find an Indian shop in your area by consulting http://thokalath.com/grocery.

INDIAN GROCERIES ONLINE

The following are sources for ordering Indian groceries online:

Kalustyan's
www.kalustyans.com

Patel Brothers
www.patelbrothersusa.com

Amazon
www.amazon.com

STARTER GROCERY LIST

I teach my cooking classes by introducing the absolute minimum ingredients to make a salad, yogurt, rice, and lentil dish. If you have these base ingredients and tools, purchased from an Indian shop or online (for recommended sources, see facing page), you can make many of the recipes in the book using vegetables, lentils, rice, and yogurt from your local grocery store. To get started, here is your shopping list; start with the smallest packet of each.

If you are interested in making dosa or idli, then purchase a medium-size bag of urad dal along with idli rice. Check pages 21 to 33 for the entire South Indian pantry and more detail on these ingredients.

INGREDIENTS

Asafetida (hing) powder

Black mustard seeds

Dried red chile peppers*

Indian green chile peppers; can substitute serrano chiles*

Curry leaves, preferably fresh

Urad dal (split black gram without skin), white in color

Chana dal (split black chickpeas without skin), yellow in color

Raw peanuts, preferably with skin; can substitute raw cashews or unsalted, roasted peanuts*

Unsweetened grated coconut (fresh, frozen, or dried)*

Tamarind paste*

Sambar powder

Basmati rice, preferably Dehraduni variety*

Red lentils (masoor dal)*

TOOLS

Masala dabba (Indian spice box or tiffin)

Tempering pot (tiny pan for frying a small amount of oil and spices)

FROM A LOCAL GROCER OR FARMER

Fresh produce

Mild-flavored oil such as canola

Plain yogurt

*You may be able to purchase these items from your local grocer as well.

ACKNOWLEDGMENTS

This book would not exist without the love, support, and guidance of a great many people in my life.

To Ma and Daddy, for your lessons in life and cooking and keeping food traditions alive in our home. For showing me India through your eyes. Thank you for everything.

To my maternal grandparents, A. Lakshminarasamma and A. L. Narasimhaiah, whose legacy lives on in many of the recipes and stories in this book, and to my paternal grandmother, Premlata Sahai, for all you taught me inside and outside the kitchen.

To my brother Vikas Agrawal, for consistently lending me your ear and giving me your best advice.

To my Arakere family. My Aunties Karen Vasudev, Shantha Kumar, Asha Janardhan, Latha Jayaram, and Usha Ramaprakash for generously taking the time to share your culinary knowledge and kitchen secrets with me. My Uncles Arakere Vasudev and Arakere Jayaram for teaching me about our family's history, and Anand Kumar, "Blue Uncle," for always rooting me on. To Sumanth Janardhan, Aparna Kumar, Kavitha Janardhan, Srini Kumar, Vijay Mohanram, Pradeep Vasudev, and Vidya Kidambi for your help and support on this project.

To Barb and Rolf Garthus for taking the time to get to know me and learn more about my family through testing and tasting my recipes.

To my agent, Stacey Glick, for your guidance and for seeing potential in me from the first day we met. To the über-talented team at Ten Speed Press for their collaboration and beautiful work: my editor Kelly Snowden, art director Kara Plikaitis, photographer Erin Scott, food stylist Lillian Kang, and copy editor Rebecca Pepper. To my Auntie Karen for hand-drawing the exquisite illustrations in this book.

I am grateful for friends who have helped me along the way as collaborators, sounding boards, or an extra set of hands at events over the years: Alana Lowe, Paul Helzer, Mia Kim, Aparna Wilder, Jennifer Piejko, Sabra Saperstein, Ben Alvarez, Diana Kuan, Cathy Erway, Laena McCarthy, Louisa Shafia, Nicole Taylor, Allison Robicelli, Lukas Volger, Dan Nishimoto, Barbara Palley, Veronica Chan, Asha Srikantiah, Sarah Kalter, Busayo Olupano, Anita Shepherd, Brian Morrison, Kara Masi, Deborah Wolf, Jason Gaspar, Clare Davies, Sangita Shah, Nik Sharma, Clay Williams, Emily Cavalier, and Joann Kim.

To Stephanie Rosemberg, Brigitte Helzer, Lakshmi Viswanathan, and T. R. Viswanathan for sharing your families recipes with me.

To my trusty group of recipe testers for your valuable feedback: Susan Larson, Nate Larson, Oscar Michel, Louisa Shafia, Kim Tarr, Aparna Wilder, Jackie Gordon, Karol Lu, David Klopfenstein, Kavitha Janardhan, Michelle Warner, Veronica Chan, Howard Walfish, Aarti Virani, Ellen Vanderlaan, Mira Evnine, Emily Dellas, Deepali Jain, Sebastian Villa, Ratna Pandit, Jeff Geady, Venkat Balasubramani, Amar Rama, Tabby Nanyonga, Sera Mathew, Sushmitha Rao, Ali Banks, Julia Cutts, Fiona Clark, Prachi Dharwadkar, Davida Persaud, Mikayla Butchart, Kahlilah Nelson, Talia Steif, Priya Edward, Archana Ram, Catalina Lopez, Maitreyi Bandlamudi, Shaheen Safdar Sutton, Rakhee Yadav, and Kalpana Sareesh.

To the readers of the ABCDs of Cooking, students at my cooking classes, and guests at my events throughout the years. I couldn't have written this without you. And to my local New York farmers, whose produce inspired many of these recipes.

Finally, thank you to my husband Ben Garthus, for joining me on this journey to Bangalore and back, and for embracing my family's food—so much, in fact, that you even made your own creations, some of which appear in this book. I love you.

INDEX

Text copyright © 2017 by Chitra Agrawal
Photographs copyright © 2017 by Erin Scott
Illustrations copyright © 2017 by Karen Vasudev

All rights reserved.

Published in the United States by Ten Speed Press, an imprint of the
Crown Publishing Group, a division of Penguin Random House LLC, New York.
www.crownpublishing.com
www.tenspeed.com

Ten Speed Press and the Ten Speed Press colophon are registered
trademarks of Penguin Random House LLC.

All photographs by Erin Scott with the exception of the photographs on
page 12, copyright © 2017 by Alana Lowe, Ethan Finklestein, and Ben Garthus,
Bangalore location and family photography © 2017 by Ben Garthus, and
author photograph page 216 copyright © 2017 by Alana Lowe

Library of Congress Cataloging-in-Publication
Names: Agrawal, Chitra, author. | Scott, Erin, photographer (expression)
Title: Vibrant India : fresh vegetarian recipes from Bangalore to Brooklyn /
by Chitra Agrawal ; photography by Erin Scott.
Description: Berkeley : Ten Speed Press, [2017] | Includes bibliographical
references and index.
Identifiers: LCCN 2016030891 (print) | LCCN 2016047723 (ebook)
Subjects: LCSH: Cooking, India. | Vegetarian cooking–India. | LCGFT:
Cookbooks.
Classification: LCC TX724.5.I4 A667 2017 (print) | LCC TX724.5.I4 (ebook) |
DDC 641.5/6360954–dc23
LC record available at https://lccn.loc.gov/2016030891

Hardcover ISBN: 9781607747345
eBook ISBN: 9781607747352
Printed in China
Design by Kara Plikaitis
10 9 8 7 6 5 4 3 2
First Edition

CHITRA AGRAWAL is a chef, culinary instructor, and food writer. She is the owner of Brooklyn Delhi, an award-winning Indian condiments line, and specializes in serving, writing about, and teaching vegetarian home cooking from India with a slant on seasonality and local ingredients. Chitra writes the popular recipe blog *The ABCDs of Cooking,* and has been featured in the *New York Times*, *Food & Wine*, *Saveur*, and *Zagat*, among others. She lives in Brooklyn, New York.